the String on a Roast Won't Catch Fire in the Oven

An A—Z Encyclopedia of Common Sense for the Newly Independent Young Adult

Candice Kohl

GYLANTIC PUBLISHING COMPANY
LITTLETON, COLORADO

Although the author has done research to ensure the accuracy and completeness of the information contained in this book, the author and publisher assume no responsibility for errors, inaccuracies, omissions or any other inconsistency herein. Data contained herein are the most complete and accurate available as this book goes to print. Please bear in mind that meanings can vary due to personal interpretation.

To order additional copies:
GYLANTIC PUBLISHING COMPANY
P.O. Box 2792
Littleton, Colorado 80161-2792
1-800-828-0113
Please add $2.00 to each order for shipping and handling

Cover design: Dannette Peterson
Printed in the United States of America by Gilliland Printing, Inc.
The text is printed with soy ink.

Library of Congress Cataloging-in-Publication-Data

Kohl, Candice, 1950-
The string on a roast won't catch fire in the oven : an a-z encyclopedia of common sense for the newly independent young adult / Candice Kohl.
p. cm.
Includes bibliographical references and index.
Summary: A survival guide for young adults out on their own, discussing apartments, job hunting, budgets, laundry, taxes, sexual relations, cars, and food.
ISBN 1-880197-07-3 : $12.95
1. Young adults–United States–Life skills guides. [1. Life skills.] I. Title.
HQ799.7.K625 1993
305.23'5–dc20 93-3961
CIP
AC

Because of Christopher;
in anticipation of Dustin

Love, Mom

Table of Contents

Dear Reader:

If you are a young adult who has just perused the Table of Contents to this book, you may be thinking, Boring. Who needs this stuff? I know all I need to know. And you may be wrong.

I accept what many say, that today's young people are far more savvy and sophisticated than previous generations. Certainly you are no exception. As well, I acknowledge that growing up is a long-term, ongoing process. But when you take that one big step toward personal independence by moving out of your parents' home, you are crossing an almost visible line of demarcation that puts you squarely in The Adult World. Whether you have recently taken that one big step or if it is still in the planning stages, when you enter The Adult World, you will find that a lot of the information and skills you acquired while still a child under your guardians' care is no longer so relevant. Additionally, you will find that a lot of the tools you need to survive as an independent adult, you have yet to learn.

It isn't your fault. So many basic skills, facts, and practices, that adults utilize daily to make their lives run smoothly would probably be considered by many mature, experienced people to be simply *common sense*. And that isn't true.

There is no mystical, mythical vein of knowledge that connects all human beings. Though *common* implies everyone can lay claim to it, and *sense* suggests an innate instinct of some kind. In truth the sort of information I have compiled in this cornucopia of facts, advice and age-old wisdom is both learned and acquired. Humans are not born knowing anything. Though an infant instinctively desires to be fed, warm and dry, unlike some other animals, there exists no ability to satisfy those needs. First the mother cares for her newborn; as the child grows and matures, the child learns from the mother.

Ideally, parents should teach their offspring to take care of themselves as adults. The problem is, in many areas older adults have been aware of certain things so long they think they have always known about them. Therefore, they assume their (nearly grown) children know about them, too—*common sense*. But we middle-aged parents are wrong. And you, our young adult children, are inadvertently being short-changed and sent out into the world when the time comes, a little less prepared than you should be.

Let's face it. Everyone who has reached the age of reason, including fairly young children, knows that in order to have clean clothes, laundry must be done. Even a preschooler probably suspects that a washing machine lies between the soiled garments she or he tosses on the bedroom floor and the clean, folded clothes that reappear in the drawers and closet. But if someone at some point doesn't explain how the machine works—how to set the water temperature, measure the detergent, sort and add the clothes—the child will never know how to do the laundry. So though doing laundry on a regular basis seems to be *common sense*, it is, in fact, a learned bit of knowledge and an acquired skill.

There's an old saying, "You can't see the forest for the trees." It means the obvious isn't always so obvious. I might not have recognized it if it were not for an incident that occurred which involved my oldest son.

At the time, he was nearing sixteen and had his temporary driver's license. Since I had listened for years to his daily recital of the listings in the "Used Auto" section of the classifieds, had endured terrifying hours of hair-raising driving lessons with him behind the wheel, had parted with a major portion of my life's savings for his car insurance, I assumed he knew enough about motor vehicles to gas up my car while I ran inside the convenience store for a gallon of milk.

Imagine my surprise when I discovered him wreaking havoc at the gas pump. First he had spent a long time simply locating the vehicle's fuel tank. Next, having found and unscrewed the gas cap, he could find no surface on which to set it without its rolling off. Credit or cash buttons on the pump were a mystery to him. I do believe he managed to figure out the pump's on/off switch, but because he didn't know how to set the nozzle lever so that the gasoline could flow and shut off automatically, he filled the gas tank manually—filled it to overflowing, so that both my rear tire and his tennies were smack in the middle of a puddle of gasoline.

You can imagine what my reaction was—probably the same as your parents' might be. Of course, I blamed my son for being stupid, ignorant, and not having a lick of common sense. Until I realized filling a car's gas tank had nothing to do with common sense. Sure, I'd been filling gas tanks for so long it seemed to me I had always known how to perform the task. But upon reflection, I recalled that I hadn't learned to fill a gas tank until I was in my mid-twenties. (It was only then, in the '70s, that self-service came into vogue, and I was informed how to fuel my own car via a helpful service station owner who shouted step-by-step instructions over a loudspeaker that, to my mortification, the entire neighborhood could hear.)

This incident got me thinking. I hadn't let my son slide behind the steering wheel of my car until he had studied for, taken and passed, the written test for a temporary license. Even before I risked my life as his passenger, I sent him first to Drivers' Education Classes. Then, in anticipation of his taking a road test, I went out with him regularly, teaching him the finer points of driving while allowing him to rack up hours of hands-on experience that would make him a better driver.

Still, I had no intention of throwing him my car keys and saying, "Have a good time," until he passed his driver's test. So why did I think he could fill up the car without first learning how it was done?

I started thinking even harder after this same son, now a few years older, went off to college and into his own apartment. It was then I took frantic phone calls and provided answers to urgent questions regarding situations I thought could be easily handled with a modicum of—you guessed it—common sense. And eventually I realized that no knowledge can be termed common sense any more than any skill can be considered instinctive.

This particular son of mine is now taking graduate courses in the School of Hard Knocks, along with innumerable bemused and befuddled classmates. I have suffered vicariously as he has suffered, my only consolation being that he, like me, and nearly everyone before us and those to come after, learns what we need to know eventually, the hard way, through personal experience.

But realizing, too, that personal experience is the most traumatic learning tool any of us utilize I have been thinking it might be easier if each generation simply clued in the next. Talking one-on-one would be best, but it isn't always possible. So how about a book? We all learned history from books, and science and math and even our Sunday School lessons. Why not a book filled with *common sense* information that will help young adults when they first go out into the world on their own?

So here you have it, a little encyclopedia of common sense knowledge. If you read it and take its advice to heart, it will smooth the way for you. If you read it and take its advice to heart, I know it will help ease your parents' minds.

C.H.K.

AAA...

APARTMENTS

If you are looking for your first apartment with or without prospective roommates, there is a good chance you will be attracted to the kind of multi-unit complex that affords the luxuries of wall-to-wall carpeting, central air, even a dishwasher. The same kind of complex also may offer the amenities of an in-house laundry room, an indoor or outdoor pool, and perhaps even a recreation building that houses saunas, exercise equipment, and table tennis. What you will be able to afford is a fourth floor walk-up containing a claw-footed bathtub and a refrigerator with a coil on the top. Do yourself a favor: don't torment yourself looking at the kind of place you are attracted to. Stick to the kind of place you can afford.

Find a little garret you can happily envision fixing up with thrift store furnishings and a lot of Con-Tact paper. The rent, at perhaps $300 a month, should fit comfortably within your budget. But don't assume you can pay the landlord $300 and move in the first of next month. Moving into a new apartment entails a lot of extra expenses that first month. To name the most critical:

First Month Plus

Besides the monthly rent, you will most certainly be asked to pay a security deposit, usually equaling a month's rent. If the rent is $300, you will have to pay your future landlord at least $600 before even considering renting a U-haul. Some places require not only a security deposit equal to a month's rent, but both the first and last month's rent in advance. That means, for this economical little apartment, you may have to pay out a full $900 in cash before you can move in.

If you pay your last month's rent in advance, you will not have to pay it in your last month of occupancy. You may have to pay an additional amount to cover any rent increases since you paid the rent in advance. In theory the security deposit will also be returned to you after you move.

To help ensure that you receive your deposit at the end of your tenancy, take a "walk-through" with your potential landlord. During the walk-through, note pre-existing conditions or problems in the unit. If there is a crack in the kitchen window, a stain on the carpeting in the corner of the front room, a hole in the bedroom wall where the doorknob was pushed into it, make sure these items are listed in writing. Determine whether or not you wish them corrected or if you can live with them. Notations should be made next to each entry specifying whether or not the landlord agrees to correct the problem and if so, an expected completion date. Two copies, signed by both the renter and rentee, should be made of this "walk-through" list. You keep one, your landlord the other. As a tenant, if problems are not attended to by their expected completion dates, you have the right to complain. If they are not attended to within a reasonable time after your complaints are made, you have the right to withhold rent until they are. Also, you can't be held liable when you vacate because you will have proof the problems existed before you moved in.

Check the state laws on tenant/landlord relationships

In some states, a landlord can retain a security deposit for a period of time after the tenant vacates. Or, you may be dealing with a real estate management firm headquartered in another state. Therefore, you should not expect your deposit returned on the same day you move out even if you are entitled to it. So don't count on your returned deposit to cover the deposit on your next abode. In fact, due to the tendency of some landlords to hold a former resident responsible for what others would consider normal upkeep, don't count on getting it back in full or ever. That way, if you do get it back it will seem like a windfall, and if you don't, you will not feel disappointed.

Utilities

Other charges that must be considered when taking a new place are hook-up and installation charges. If you are a first time utility customer, you may be asked to pay a refundable deposit. Even though the electricity was on when you originally toured that cute little cubby hole you now intend to call home, before you actually move in you must call the utilities and inform them of your date of occupancy. Utilities are the electric, gas and even phone companies. They will not only begin charging you for your gas usage as of your first date of occupancy, they may charge you additional fees. For instance, if the gas has to be hooked up, you will find an additional, one-time service fee on your first monthly bill. And even though you bought your own phone at a discount department store and there are jacks in each room of your new apartment, the telephone company will charge you a one-time installation fee on your first bill in addition to the normal monthly service charge.

Moving Expenses

You may also incur moving expenses. If you are moving any distance, you have to pick up recently acquired furniture, or if you have so many belongings at your mother's house you can't manage to haul them all from one place to the other in several back-and-forth car trips, you may have to rent a van or trailer. Fees for such vehicles are usually hourly, but a refundable deposit may be required up front; gasoline for the vehicle must also be purchased. Be sure to allow for these expenses during that crucial first month on your own.

You may think you can get by cheaply because your buddy has a pick-up and has volunteered to help move your possessions to the new apartment. You may also have other friends willing to help load and unpack. But free laborers expect to be nourished, so consider the cost of beer, soft drinks and pizzas that you will have to buy to feed your friends.

It is cheaper to move with friends helping, but there are still costs involved. Don't ignore these costs, or you may end up cash short.

Incidentals

So you have your old bed and inflatable chairs and a CD player. More than enough to get you started, you think. Think again, and allow for the incidentals that will eat into your first month's budget: a shower curtain and rings, mop, pail and broom, can opener, hot pads, toilet paper, towels. These are things that may have been provided for you, either in your dorm or at your parents' house. Now you will need your own, and you will not be able to do long without them.

Allow for the cost of these incidentals. Of course, you can't ask for some things, but wherever possible try to liberate extras from long-standing households run by your mother, grandmother or mothers of friends. The more you can score for free, the better off you will be. Worry about tasteful decorating when you are a little older and more financially secure.

The Lease

A final note regarding the new apartment: Usually you will be required to sign a lease. A lease is a legally binding contract between you and the landlord. Leases usually run for a year's time beginning with the date you take occupancy. Sometimes they specify that the monthly rent can't be raised during the course of that year, but sometimes they don't. This allows the landlord to raise the rent, but prevents you from moving. Always it states that you, the renter, are responsible for the monthly rent of your unit for the period of the lease.

What this means is, six months into your lease should you get both a whopping raise at work and discover an available apartment in a complex with a pool, you can't simply give notice on your little garret and move out. Because you are responsible for the remaining six months' rent, you must choose one of the following options: Pay six months' rent to your landlord in a lump sum before moving; pay the rent on your old apartment while paying rent on your new one until the old lease expires; find someone to sublet your current apartment who will pay the monthly rent to you, which you will then forward to the landlord; or find someone to rent your apartment immediately upon your own planned departure, and make arrangements with your landlord for the new renters to complete the terms of your unexpired lease.

Certain portions of a lease may be negotiable and revised before you sign. For instance, you may ask for and receive a six month lease instead of the standard one year. Or, you may be able to forego the security deposit on your flat if you agree to mow the lawn and shovel the walks.

Leases are not actually bad or ominous things. Providing you don't break the conditions of the lease (e.g., keeping a pet when pets are not allowed, disturbing your neighbors' peace by practicing with your rock band till the wee hours of the morning) you are guaranteed a place to live for the specified time. Usually the lease outlines things the landlord must provide for you, such as working laundry facilities, secured parking, etc. During periods when occupancy of rental units is low, you may be able to negotiate additional perks into the contract: a free month's rent, free heat, free cable television, or discounts on any of the above. But in order to ensure you receive these "incentives," you must make certain they are written into the lease.

ESTIMATED COSTS OF THE MOVE

Up front expenses:		
	First month's rent	$ 300.
	Last month's rent	300.
	Security deposit	300.
	Up front cash needed	$ 900.
Other possible expenses:		
	Rental of U-haul	$ 60.
	Pizza and drinks for helpers	30.
	Utilities/Phone deposits	100.
Total moving expenses		$1,090.

Getting your own first apartment can be fun and exiting; that initial scent of freedom is always heady. It can be not only intoxicating but as expensive as the rarest of perfumes. Be prepared for the cost and cut corners where you can.

Summary

✔ The cost of acquiring your first apartment includes more than just the monthly rent. Some of the additional expenses are security deposit, utility installation fees, utility deposits, moving costs, household goods.

✔ A lease is a legally binding contract between you and the landlord. The lease binds you to pay rent for the specified period and to maintain the apartment. The landlord is also obligated to perform certain services. Understand the terms and conditions before you sign a lease.

Recommended Reading

Waldman, David. *How to Negotiate a Lease on Your Terms: Guerilla Tactics for Renting an Apartment, House or Trailer Home...* Deer Park, NY: Forms Man, Inc., 1991.

BBB...

BUDGETS

Everybody feels rich on payday, but it is a rare worker who is paid on a daily basis. Few are paid weekly anymore. Most of us, whether we work full or part-time, are paid on an average of twice a month. When you cash your paycheck or deposit it in a bank account, it is difficult, seeing that wad of bills in your hand or that lofty balance in your checkbook, not to feel a giddy, impulsive urge to embark on a spending spree. But restrain yourself. The amount of money that makes you feel wealthy today would probably seem meager if divided by the number of days that lay between now and next payday. It would look even smaller if you subtracted the expenses you know it must cover during that same period. Yet that is what you must do.

This is called budgeting. Budgeting is an unnatural experience. It goes against every innate characteristic we are born with. A human being desires immediate gratification from the moment she or he makes an entrance into the world. An infant wants to be fed, warm, comfortable and most of all, happy. In our society, especially as we grow older, often great quantities of money are required to keep us fed, warm, comfortable and happy. Instinctively, we wish to spend those quantities of money—on handsome clothes,

fast cars, beautiful jewelry, luxury vacations, good food in fine restaurants, top quality stereo components, and big screen televisions.

Not spending money on these self-indulgent, instantly gratifying things, but instead setting aside money for necessities such as rent, utilities and groceries, is called budgeting. Since budgeting goes against all we desire, it is a hateful business. It is so hateful, in fact, that many young adults (and even quite a number of older ones), refuse to do it. They see a designer dress or Italian suit in a shop window and promptly purchase it. They entertain, they travel, they buy home furnishings, usually on credit if they can obtain it. Though they are immediately gratified, satisfied human beings, a brief time later they find themselves cash short, either because their bank accounts are overdrawn or because they have so many revolving credit bills their monthly cash outlay exceeds their incomes. Then they must pay a financial counselor to help them consolidate their loans, sell off belongings of value, perhaps even file for bankruptcy.

As a newly emancipated young adult, you don't want to head down the delightfully scenic road to financial ruin. To avoid this particular route, you must budget.

How Do You Budget?

In advance, not after the fact.

First of all, develop a practical mind set: You are twenty, not forty, and though you would like to have the same kind of trappings you had while living in your parents' house, don't expect to obtain them as soon as you move out on your own. Your parents' furniture is fine and will last long enough to become antiques. Your furniture should likely be as old as antiques, but probably classified as junk. Your father buys his cars for their comfort and style. If you can afford one at all, your car should be purchased because it can still get from point A to point B without breaking down enroute. Your mother gives fashionable parties with catered hors d'oeuvres trays and professionally arranged floral center pieces. You should host only B.Y.O. parties and give small, intimate dinners featuring spaghetti and garlic bread.

Once you have a practical mind-set with reasonable expectations far beneath those of your middle-aged parents, you are well on your way to successful budgeting. Knowing you can't have it all or even the best of anything, you will not be so tempted to indulge yourself. Knowing that your time will come and your income and standard of living will increase and improve with the passing years will help ease the pain of a budget's bite.

To begin budgeting while you are still solvent (instead of in the middle of a financial crisis), you must plan. Do this by taking out paper, pencil, and a calculator (see example on page 10).

- ✍ Write down all your unavoidable monthly expenses, rounding off the figures.
- ✍ Write down average weekly costs for groceries, gasoline or bus fare, pantyhose, contact lens solution, entertainment—all the things you spend money on routinely but which vary in cost from week to week. Get an average monthly figure for each of these items by multiplying them by four.
- ✍ Consider infrequent (annual or semi-annual) expenses, such as insurance premiums or college tuition. Divide annual billings by twelve, semi-annual by six. This will give you an idea of how much of your income should be set aside per month so that you will have funds in reserve to pay these infrequent bills when they come due.
- ✍ Determine how much you have or intend to spend annually on clothing, vehicle maintenance, and possibly health, dental and eye care. Divide these yearly, projected figures by twelve to determine how much of your income should be set aside or allotted monthly to cover these necessities.

Monthly Budget—March

		Monthly totals	
Monthly net income			$909
Monthly expenses			
Rent	300		
Gas & Electric	50		
Telephone	20		
Car payment	75		
Subtotal		445	
Weekly expenditures			
Groceries	40		
Gasoline (or bus fare)	10		
Guitar lesson	10		
Entertainment	15		
Weekly total	75		
Each week X 4 1/3= monthly total		325	
Semi-annual expenditures divide by 6			
Car insurance $300/6	50		
Tuition/Books $300/6	50		
Subtotal		100	
Anticipated annual expenditures per month			
Clothing $600/12	50		
Contact lens $300/12	25		
Subtotal		75	
Total Expenses			945
Reserve for savings or			0
Cut monthly expenses by			$ 36

Ideas for cutting expenses:

1) cut clothing costs $5/month—shop second-hand stores

2) cut food costs $5/week—less prepared foods, use coupons buy generic stuff

3) cut entertainment $10/month—go to $1.50 movies, videos

Now, add together these amounts which reflect fixed monthly bills and usual monthly expenses as well as moneys to be set aside regularly to cover infrequent expenditures. Next, subtract this total amount from your monthly, fixed, net income[1].

These figures represent a basic monthly budget that may be broken down into a weekly or per pay period budget, or expanded into an annual fiscal plan. Henceforth, when you are paid, go to your bank:

- ✔ deposit funds to cover your rent and other bills
- ✔ take money out for groceries and other cash purchases
- ✔ put money into a separate savings account so that you have enough funds in reserve to cover future expenditures such as tuition or new eye glasses

---

If your employer offers automatic payroll deductions to be deposited into a credit union savings account, take advantage of it. Your money will go directly into your savings account without you having the opportunity to spend it. Many companies are members of a credit union. These institutions are similar to banks. The main difference is that only employees of the company and their family members can belong to the credit union. Frequently, savings rates will be slightly higher at a credit union than a traditional bank.

If You Don't Budget

At your age and in your circumstances, it is doubtful your income will exceed you expenses. But hopefully your income will be equal to your expenses. If it isn't, you can't ignore the difference. Don't disregard the fact you will be receiving a semi-annual insurance premium billing four months from

1 Net means take-home pay, as opposed to gross, which refers to your actual salary before taxes, F.I.C.A., insurance and union dues are withheld.

now. If you have the attitude, "I'll worry about it when the time comes," and don't set aside the money for your auto insurance between now and then, you will not have it. When you don't have it, you will have to stop driving, perhaps sell your car. Or you will be tempted to borrow the money to pay your premium, and then you will have not only the next six month premium to save for but the last six month premium to pay bay back.

If Your Budget Doesn't Balance

What can you do if your budget doesn't balance? Earn more or spend less. The more difficult option of the two at your stage of life would be to earn more. If you are a full-time worker already, you may want to start looking for a better paying job. You may want to try putting in some overtime. Or you may want to consider moonlighting. If you are still in school and working only part-time, you may also want to start looking for a better paying job. Or you may want to try getting some additional hours at work. But trying to balance your budget by increasing your income isn't an option you can readily control. Perhaps you are not yet qualified to land a better paying position. Or perhaps there is no overtime available. Or perhaps you can't fit additional working hours into your schedule.

Each dollar you cut from expenses brings you a dollar closer to balancing your budget. But each extra dollar of earnings can only be considered after-tax. Therefore, a dollar less spent is greater than a dollar earned.

Food

The only remaining option that you can control is to spend less. At first thought you may consider it impossible, but trust me, spending less is always possible. The easiest expense to cut is food. Do you buy one-serving convenience foods, such as frozen entrees? *Don't.* Cook from scratch. Convenience is expensive. Do you buy lunch out, at school or work? *Stop it;* brown bag it. If you are in college and food tickets for the cafeteria are included with your room and board, even if the food is less than grand cuisine take all the meals you can at the cafeteria. If you still live in the same town as your family, drop by to visit frequently, and make some of these visits near meal time.

Clothing

Other ways to cut down are in your clothing purchases. Stay out of the malls unless you know ahead of time that certain stores are having special sales. Otherwise, shop at discount designer outlets where you will be able to buy good clothing at very reasonable prices, even if they are irregulars. Be sure to examine garments for noticeable flaws before you buy. Shop at thrift and second-hand stores, where a blouse can cost fifty cents and a man's suit $10. When you are older you will want to dress well and fashionably, and you will probably be able to lay out the big bucks to do it. When you are younger you can dress frugally but funky by laying out only some of your hard earned pennies.

Transportation

We live in a mobile society, so transportation costs always figure into a budget unless you are lucky enough to live within walking distance of your work or school. If you are not that lucky, ask yourself: Do I really need a car? How much can I spend on oil and maintenance each month? How much can I afford to spend on auto insurance? Could I get by using public transportation and taking a cab only on special occasions? How about a bicycle? It isn't the '50s anymore, when only children pedaled their Schwinns around town. A good, ten-speed racer may cost as much as a third-hand auto, but maintenance and insurance costs are practically nil. You can save a great deal by not owning a motorized vehicle.

Living arrangements

Last but not least, if you live alone do you have room for, and could you tolerate, a roommate? By bringing another person into your apartment, the rent and all utilities would be cut in half. A loss of some privacy could well be worth a reduction by half of your housing-related expenses.

Other thoughts

This doesn't mean that, if you are living tight, you can't ever treat yourself to something frivolous. Everyone needs to indulge themselves once in a while—it is good for the spirit and soul. But not every payday.

If the budget you compiled shows you not to be cash short but cash heavy, you are free to indulge yourself a little more excessively. A warning: Though you have extra funds today, tomorrow you may not. Life has a way of throwing curves—unexpected medical bills, tuition increases, your only television set blacking out and requiring expensive repairs. It is best to plan for such unexpected expenditures, as they are inevitable. Saving for a rainy day has become an old adage because it is sound advice.

If you have extra cash coming in every month, you may wish to make your cash grow. You can do this by opening a savings account or investing in tax-deferred retirement accounts or mutual funds. [See chapter KKK...]

Summary

- ✔ Budgeting means living within your income and spending less than you earn.
- ✔ Work out a basic budget. Estimate all your regular expenses.
- ✔ Compare your monthly estimated expenses to your monthly net income.

- ✔ Take action now if your expenses are greater than your income. You must reduce expenses or increase income. It is quicker and easier to cut expenses.
- ✔ If you have an excess, you have the power to indulge yourself, save more, or invest.

Recommended Reading

Clason, George S., *The Richest Man in Babylon.* New York: Plume, 1955.

Lawrence, Judy. *Common Cents: The Complete Money Management Workbook.* Homewood, IL: Dow Jones-Irwin, 1986.

Sloane, Leonard. *Book of Personal Finance.* New York: Times Books, 1992.

BBB...

CCC...

CHECKING ACCOUNT

Checks

Checks are not only for cashing, they are for paying debts and are a wonderfully convenient invention. Checks enable you to pay bills without personally going to the stores and companies you owe; to make purchases even if you are not carrying enough cash to pay for an item; and to record much of your spending. But if you write checks, please remember that having blank checks in your vinyl checkbook holder doesn't mean you still have money in your bank account.

Here are some other things you should know about opening a checking account, writing checks, keeping a checkbook, and maintaining the account.

Opening A Checking Account

When you decide to open a checking account, shop around. Having a checking account costs money. Some banks and thrifts require keeping as much as $250 as an untouched balance before they give you "free checking," while others, such as credit unions, pay interest on your checking account balance no matter how small that balance is. Look for a financial institution that is convenient for you in terms of location, but look for your best deal as well.

Opening a checking account costs money. First, you must have funds to deposit. Then you must buy checks. Designer checks are pretty, but they may cost more than plain ones. Checks with carbonless paper duplicates provide an immediate and very handy record of all the checks you write, but they are usually twice as expensive as plain checks. Still, since many banks no longer send customers their canceled checks on a monthly basis, the duplicate checks may be worth the additional expense. Also, personal checks ordered in large quantities may be cheaper per check, but the original outlay will be costly. You could end up moving—and reordering additional checks with your new address—before you use up the quantity you first purchased.

REORDERING CHECKS

Check reorders are one of the biggest markup items for banks. You can save money by buying personalized checks elsewhere.

Write for a price comparison:

Checks In The Mail, P.O. Box 7802, Irwindale, CA 91706
Custom Direct, P.O. Box 145439, Cincinnati, OH 45250
Current, P.O. Box 19000 Colorado Springs, CO 80935
Image Checks, P.O. Box 548, Little Rock, AR 72203

Writing A Check

Let's assume now that you have your own account and your own book of blank checks. How do you write a check?

- In the upper right hand corner on the date line, write in today's date.
- On the line headed Pay to the order of ... write the name of the person or company to whom you are writing the check.

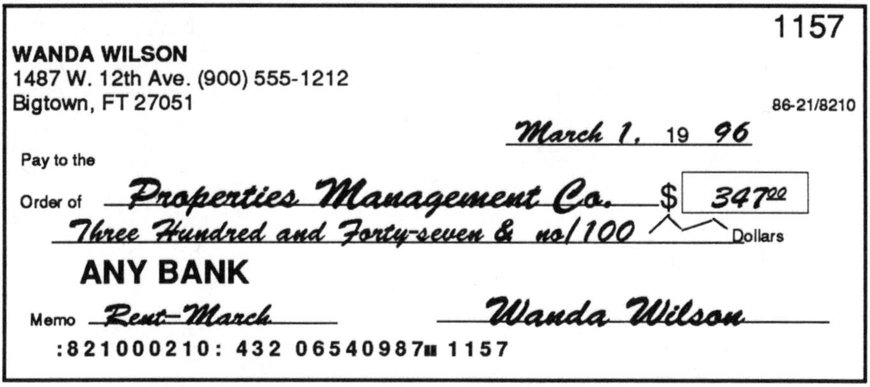
1157

WANDA WILSON
1487 W. 12th Ave. (900) 555-1212
Bigtown, FT 27051

86-21/8210

March 1, 19 96

Pay to the Order of Properties Management Co. $ 347.00

Three Hundred and Forty-seven & no/100 Dollars

ANY BANK

Memo Rent—March Wanda Wilson

:821000210: 432 06540987⑈ 1157

- Following that line, in the little box headed with a dollar sign, write the amount of the check in numerals.
- On the next line, usually followed by the word *dollars*, write the amount of dollars in cursive. Except write the decimal (cents) as a fraction. For example $23.47 would be written as: Twenty-three and 47/100. Follow the dollar amount by a squiggly line that continues right to the printed word *dollars*. This prevents someone from increasing the amount you have written and cashing the check for the higher amount.
- On the line in the bottom right hand corner of the check, sign your name as it is listed on your account.
- If you have a memo line in the bottom left hand corner of your checks, you may write a brief reminder of how the money was spent. For example: Car repairs, groceries, Mom's gift.
- When you write a personal check at a store, you will usually have to provide two forms of identification, such as a driver's license and a credit card, work or school identification card or guaranteed check card. If you don't drive, you may be able to obtain a picture identification card from your state's Department of Motor Vehicles. Or, if you have a passport, carry it with you for purposes of identification. (See chapter EEE... for how to obtain a passport.)

✍ Whenever you write a check, record it immediately in your check register. The register is that pad of blank, lined pages that fits above your blank checks in your checkbook. Immediately record in the register the following information: the number of the check; check date; the name of the party to whom you wrote the check; what the check was for; and, the amount of the check.

✍ Immediately subtract that amount from your balance and if applicable, note that the check is tax deductible in the space provided in the register.

You may sometimes wish to write a personal check in order to receive cash. Certain stores, taverns, credit unions and other places that you frequent regularly will allow you to do this. Instead of writing the name of the tavern or the company you work for on the *Pay to the Order of* line, write the word *CASH* in capitals. Complete the rest of the check as previously described. Never write a check to "cash" in advance. Someone may be able to cash the check if they find it.

Endorsing A Check

If you receive a check from someone else made out in your name, in order to cash or deposit it endorse it on the back. Flip the check over and on the left hand edge, width-wise, write your name in cursive. Be sure to keep your signature within one inch of the edge, because banks use scanning equipment that requires endorsement signatures to be in that precise area. If you are going to deposit the check in your account add "For Deposit Only" and your account number. This will prevent someone from cashing your endorsed check if they find it.

Deposit

When you make a deposit to your account, either direct,[1] by mail, or in person (your bank's customer service representative can and should describe the options to you when you open your account), be sure to note the deposit in your check register. Add that amount to your previous balance.

Insufficient Funds (Bounced Check)

If you write a check in an amount higher than your actual account balance, that check will not clear. When a check doesn't clear it is called a bad check because it isn't good for the amount written. Your financial institution will notify you in writing if you have written a bad check on an overdrawn account, expecting you:

- ✔ to deposit enough additional funds to cover the check, and
- ✔ to pay an amount up to $15 for the inconvenience you have caused them.

Also, the person or company to whom you wrote the bad check will be fined up to $15 by their financial institution for trying to deposit a bad check to their own account, even though it was not their fault you had insufficient funds. In turn, particularly if the party involved is a company rather than a personal friend, the recipient of your bouncing check will charge you for the fee imposed on them by their own bank. The following example illustrates how costly writing bad checks can be.

THE COST OF WRITING BAD CHECKS

You have written four checks for household bills ($25, $35, $12 and $28) totaling $100.

You only have $3.75 in your checking account.

Original payments (four checks)	$100
Minimum bank charge for four bad checks	$ 60
Minimum charge from recipients of bad checks	$ 60
Total cost to you of writing the four bad checks	$ 220

1 A direct deposit is when your wages are deposited directly into your personal bank account by your employer. You don't receive a check on payday; your bank account balance simply increases by the amount due you for your net wages.

On the other hand, should you attempt to ignore the situation by not covering the amount of the checks you wrote and not paying the fees, you could end up in court. The result would eventually be the cost of the initial checks, compounded fees, additional fines, legal and court costs.

So remember, a bad check that bounces for lack of funds can be an expensive piece of work. *Don't write checks that exceed the balance in your account.*

Stop Payment

If you should ever write a check for a product or service that you subsequently don't receive or which you feel is defective, you may wish to stop payment. You can do this by notifying your bank, providing the check has not yet cleared. When it does come in, the bank will not honor it. However, this service can cost you up to $15, so you don't want to stop payment on a check unless it is for a sizable amount and no other recourse is available to you.

Balancing Your Checking Account

Every month your financial institution will send you a statement detailing the activity in your checking account. Your statement will list the checks you have written that have cleared your account in the order the bank received them, not in numerical order. As soon as possible after receiving your statement review it, making adjustments so that the bank statement and your check register agree.

- ✍ Compare the bank statement transactions with the transactions you have recorded in your check register.
- ✍ Put a check-mark (✔) in your check register next to the number of each check that cleared the bank.
- ✍ Total the sum of all recorded checks which are still outstanding, i.e. have not cleared the bank yet.

✍ Verify that all deposits you made and recorded in your check register have been recorded by the bank.

Bank Statement

DATE	DESCRIPTION	WITHDRAWALS	DEPOSIT	BALANCE
7/13	WITHDRAWAL AT ATM	10.00		
	CHECK 1238	59.47		146.20
7/16	DEPOSIT MADE		467.34	613.54
7/20	CHECK 1241	347.00		
	CHECK 1237	20.22		
	CHECK 1240	25.40		220.92
7/22	SERVICE CHARGE	9.00		211.92
TOTAL WITHDRAWALS/DEPOSITS		468.09	467.34	
ENDING BALANCE				211.92

Checkbook Register

NUMBER	DATE	DESCRIPTION	AMOUNT OF CHECK	T	AMOUNT OF DEPOSIT	BALANCE
						215.67
1237	7/11	Telephone	20.22			195.45
1238		Grocery store	59.47			135.98
	7/13	ATM	10.—			125.98
	7/16	Deposit			467.34	593.32
1239	7/18	Car payment	132.14			461.18
1240	7/18	m/c payment	25.40			435.78
1241		Rent	347.00			88.78
1242		Power Co.	32.71			56.07
	7/24	Deposit			15.00	71.07
	7/27	Service Charge(bank statement)	9.00			62.07

✍ Deduct from your check register balance any service charges or fees which you hadn't recorded.

✍ Make sure your automatic teller machines (ATM) withdrawals agree with the bank's record.

Now you are ready to reconcile your bank account. Fill in the following information.

Bank Reconciliation Form

Checks: Outstanding	
Check #	Amount $
1239	132.14
1242	32.71
Total	$ 164.85

Bank Balance from Statement	$ 211.92
Add: Deposits not included in this statement	$ 15.00
Total	$ 226.92
Subtract: Checks outstanding	$ 164.85
Revised Bank Balance	$ 62.07
Checkbook Balance	$ 71.07
Add: Deposits not entered in checkbook	$
Total	$
Subtract: Withdrawals not entered in checkbook *Service Charge*	$ 9.00
Revised Checkbook Balance	$ 62.07

The final tally on your reconciliation should match the balance you now have in your check register. If you are a few cents, or even a few dollars, off you can either ignore the discrepancy or review your arithmetic. If you are really off, you had better start all over again, perhaps going back a month or two in your records. You might even contact the bank and ask that a customer service representative walk you through your personal records and theirs until the mistake is identified. Big discrepancies mean someone has made a mistake and though, more times than not, that someone is the bank customer, on occasion it is the bank itself. Remember, a bank isn't really an *it* at all, but a company comprised of human beings who work with computers. Human beings, even if they are bank employees, can make mistakes on the job, and computers sometimes glitch.

In any case, be sure you balance your checkbook monthly. Hidden fees, in particular service charges and ATM withdrawals, decrease the balance in your account daily. If you don't reconcile your records with the bank's, you could find yourself overdrawn and bouncing checks.

Keep your monthly statements, canceled checks and/or duplicate check copies. (A shoe box will do.) You may need a copy of a check to prove a purchase, and you will need statements and/or copies to prove deductions on your income taxes. For tax purposes, keep your bank records for at least three years.

Automatic Teller Machines (ATMs)

A note about cash cards, ATMs, and how they work: Often you can obtain a cash card when you open a checking account. Such a card will enable you to make various transactions, including withdrawals from ATMs. To use a cash card you slide it into the appropriate slot in the machine, enter your personal identification number, and follow the ATM's instructions to perform the type of transaction you desire. Many people use these machines to get quick cash.

If you routinely take money out of your checking account via an automatic teller machine, *be sure you enter the withdrawals* in your check register or else you will think you have more money than you actually do. ATM withdrawals are immediate. Also, be aware that teller machine privileges are rarely free. Though you may be allowed several free teller machine transactions per month, additional transactions may cost you about fifty cents each. These fees must also be subtracted from your account.

Summary

✔ Checking accounts are a convenience that save you time and make bill paying efficient.

- ✔ There are costs involved in obtaining and maintaining a checking account.
- ✔ Record all transactions you make at the time you make them.
- ✔ Reconcile your bank balance as soon as you receive the bank statement.
- ✔ Avoid writing bad checks by maintaining proper records.
- ✔ Keep bank records for at least three years for tax purposes.

Recommended Reading

Fitzgibbon, Dan. *All About Your Money*. New York: Atheneum, 1984.

DDD...

DEBT AND CREDIT

Credit cards have almost become a necessity in our culture. Like a checkbook but even better, they allow you to make purchases when you are not carrying enough cash and to order products, even theater or concert tickets, over the telephone. They are also great for emergencies. Say, for instance, you have a breakdown during a road trip. Your bank credit card can satisfy your hotel, meal and car repair bills. They can help you establish a credit rating so that in the future you will be able to obtain bank loans for major purchases, such as a new car or a house. They also serve as identification when writing checks.

Credit Cards

There are different kinds of credit cards.

- ✔ Individual store credit cards—used only at the store named on the card.
- ✔ Oil company credit cards—used only at affiliated service stations.
- ✔ Long distance telephone services credit cards—they enable you to make long distance calls from public phones

without having to pump a pocketful of change into the phone on site.

✔ Specific catalog merchandise credit cards—used to order goods by phone from a particular catalog house.

✔ Bank credit cards—used for purchases or rentals of merchandise or services on credit from thousands of participating stores and companies, not only across the country but around the world.

I'll, however, only discuss bank credit cards here since they are the most common and widely-used form of credit card. The two major bank cards are Visa and MasterCard. In addition to shopping convenience, they enable you to get cash advances from banks and certain ATMs.

Bank credit cards are wonderful things, and the thousands of banks that issue them desperately want you to own one. That's because they are even more wonderful for card issuers than for card holders. They make millions of dollars annually for the banks that issue them.

While you were still in your senior year of high school, you probably started receiving applications for bank cards from various financial institutions. Now that you are on your own, you will receive many, many more. There is a difference between the kind of bank cards offered dependent students and those offered independent, self-supporting adults. The first kind require a student's parents to co-sign. If such a card is issued and the principal card holder, the student, doesn't pay the monthly bill, the parents are liable for the charge account balance. Although ideally these cards could come in handy for students attending school far from home, most parents, I am sure, are reluctant to let their college-aged children have them. Why? Because credit issued to a person never held accountable for payment is credit asking to be abused.

The kind of bank card you may be urged to apply for now that you are an independent adult will not require co-signers. You alone will be responsible for its use and payment. If you do apply, you will be required to supply information regarding your employment and banking history. If you are deemed reliable and have no bad credit in your past, like defaulting on a record club membership or skipping out of an apartment without paying your last month's rent, you will probably be issued a bank card.

Now you will start paying.

Usually there is an immediate annual fee of anywhere from $15 to $25. If you charge items and don't pay them off in full with every bill you receive, you will pay interest on the balance owed, somewhere between 12% to 22% annually. When you consider that the average regular savings account pays less than 5% interest and that the average Certificate of Deposit pays about 3-4% as of this writing, you get an idea of how staggering the interest rates on credit card balances are. These rates are high to help cover the losses on the cards of those who default on their loans.

Credit Card Advice

My advice is, don't get a bank credit card until you are at least in your early twenties and have a secure, steady job. When you do decide to get a bank credit card, shop around just as you should for a checking account. Dozens of banks in every city and town issue the two major bank cards; it's a competitive business, so some offer better rates than others. Sometimes the business section of the local newspaper will carry lists of banks with the lowest credit card rates. A big New York City bank may offer you a credit line of a thousand dollars, but their annual fee and interest rate will also be among the highest. A local bank might allow you only a $300 line of credit, but they may charge no annual fee and their interest rate could be as low as 12%.

If you want a credit card for emergencies, which is not a bad idea, keep it for emergencies. Don't carry it with you so that you are tempted to indulge in purchases you can't really afford.

If your income is steady and you decide to get a charge card to help establish a credit rating, pay off your balance every month. Use the card infrequently, for convenience. Say you are in the mall and you find a to-die-for leather jacket on sale, half price. Charge it, but pay the bill in full when it arrives. There will be no interest charges tacked on, and you won't begin accumulating a large debt.

TO CHARGE OR NOT TO CHARGE

If you are tempted to use your credit card for nonemergencies, deduct the charge from your check register balance to reserve money for the payment.

If this leaves you with a negative balance, *you can't afford the item.*

Budget counselors are swamped with young adults, single and married, who have charged numerous bank and store credit cards to the limit. Unable to make all the monthly payments they owe and still have money for living expenses, they are desperate to avoid bankruptcy. If you don't want to end up in the same boat with them, delay getting credit cards as long as possible.

Unpaid balances have a way of growing. Let's take a look:

Suppose you go on a little shopping spree and use your bank card to charge purchases totaling $300. Things are a little tighter than you expected them to be when the bill arrives, and you can't pay off the balance in full. In fact, it is all you can do to make the minimum payment of $15. Do you think next month's bill will be for $285? Guess again: You have interest charges of 1.5% a month, compounded annually at 18%.

If you continue making minimum payments of $15, this is what a composite view of your monthly bills would look like:

Minimum Payment	Applied to Balance	Interest Paid	Balance
			$300.00
$15.00	$15.00	$0	285.00
15.00	10.72	4.28	274.28
15.00	10.89	4.11	263.39
15.00	11.05	3.95	252.23
15.00	11.21	3.79	241.13
15 00	11.39	3.61	229.74
....	....	....	....

If you pay the $300 in full when you get the bill, you will not pay any interest.

Do you see where you are going here? At this rate, it will take twenty-four months to pay off this bill and those original $300 purchases will end up costing you $353. If you continue to make purchases, even in small amounts of $20 or $40, they will add to the principal. The interest against the increased amount will be larger, and paying off your account will seem a near impossibility.

Cash Advances

Also, if you take cash advances against your bank credit card or you write checks against your credit card (these are special checks from the Visa or MasterCard company, not your personal bank account checks), a percentage of any payment you make will go specifically toward the cash advances. For instance, if you have a balance of $500 for purchases and another $150 for cash advances or checks, these two balances are maintained separately. Your one, monthly payment of $50 will be divided, perhaps $40 going toward the purchase balance and $10 toward the cash. It is very near to having two completely separate credit loans to pay off every month. Often, interest rates on cash advances are higher by a percentage point or more than interest on purchases.

DO YOU NEED TO HAVE A CREDIT CARD?

If you want an easy way to establish a good credit record, a credit card may be the answer. A credit card is handy when you travel and the good credit record you establish through the prudent and wise use of your card will make obtaining a car or home mortgage loan a little easier. The key word is *good* credit. So use your credit card with the future in mind.

Guaranteed Bank Card

There is still another type of bank credit card. It is called a guaranteed bank card. Certain banks offer them, and because they have the same name as the two major bank cards used in this country, I don't believe a store clerk could recognize them as being different from any other. But they are.

When you get a guaranteed (or "secured") bank card, you deposit with the bank a specified sum (perhaps $250). You can't make any withdrawals from this account; it is there to guarantee your line of credit. You can use your bank card to charge purchases up to the amount you have already deposited with that bank. Though you have paid in advance, you still have to make payments to cover your charge purchases. But after your have proven you will pay the balance you run up on your card, your original deposit may again become available to you to do with as you choose.

People get guaranteed bank cards for one of two reasons: to establish credit if they have no other option available, or to re-establish good credit after having established bad credit.

Other Ways to Establish Credit

There are other ways to establish credit besides the use of credit cards. Safe methods include taking out magazine subscriptions and paying the annual fees in installments. You might also be able to take out a small bank loan. But these days, if you don't already have a savings account at that institution that contains more money than you wish to borrow, it is unlikely you would be able to get such a loan. The one type of lending institution that would grant a loan to someone without either credit or solid financial resources is a financial services company. My advice is, *don't* borrow from these companies. Such firms cater to those who can't obtain loans from more traditional financial institutions like banks or savings and loans, but their interest rates are extremely high and they give no quarter to those who fall on hard times and get behind in their payments.

CREDIT UNIONS

If you belong to a credit union, don't forget it when looking for credit cards or loans. Rates will probably be somewhat more favorable than bank credit cards or loans. More important, it is often easier to build a good relationship with your credit union than with a bank.

Safeguarding Credit Cards

Once you have credit cards, remember they are as good as cash. Unlike personal checks, when you use them for purchases, no additional identification is required. Therefore, if you lose your wallet or someone steals your cards, it is possible that some one other than yourself could run up large bills against your account. If your credit cards are ever lost or stolen, report this information to the credit card companies immediately. *Always keep your credit card number(s) and where to call if it is lost or stolen separate from your billfold or purse.*

In some states the card holder can't be held liable for anything beyond a specified amount, for example $50 per card, if the stolen cards are reported. Still, depending upon how many cards are stolen from you, that minimal amount could end up becoming a tidy sum for which you are responsible. So I recommend buying credit card insurance.

Credit Card Insurance

Years ago I would have advised against credit card insurance. I thought if you called in lost or stolen cards to the companies that issued them, you would be safe enough. Then I was robbed at gunpoint while on vacation. It happened on a Saturday night, I was in a strange city in a state I'd never before visited. The thief not only got my cards but absolutely everything in terms of identification. Fortunately, only weeks earlier in what I had immediately thought to be a moment of weakness, I had purchased credit card insurance. Was I glad I had! One phone call to a twenty-four hour 800 number, and they immediately canceled all my credit cards so I was not liable for a cent. Credit card insurance is inexpensive and now, I feel, well worth the cost. If you have more than one card, I recommend you buy insurance, too.

Summary

- ✔ Credit cards are costly in terms of annual fees and interest.
- ✔ If you don't have the funds to cover a check written for a non-emergency item, you should forego making the purchase.
- ✔ Use credit and particularly credit cards only when necessary.
- ✔ Limit credit cards to one all-purpose card.
- ✔ Protect your card from being stolen and consider credit card insurance.

Recommended Reading

Bley, Kenneth Winter. *Getting Out From Under: The Complete Guide to Controlling Your Finances, Negotiating Your Creditors, and Emerging Debt-Free.* Chicago: Consumer's Press, Inc., 1991.

Clason, George S., *The Richest Man in Babylon.* New York: Plume, 1955.

Fitzgibbon, Dan. *All About Your Money.* New York: Atheneum, 1984.

Landau, Elaine. *The Smart Spending Guide for Teens.* New York: J. Messner, 1982.

Sloane, Leonard. *Book of Personal Finance.* New York: Times Books, 1992.

DDD...

EEE

EXCURSIONS AND TRAVEL

You are spending the night at (ahem!) a friend's house. No big deal. If you take along your own toothbrush it might come in handy, but your own home will survive your absence for an additional twelve to twenty-four hours.

But now you have been invited to your boss' house on the shore for a three-day weekend. You have goldfish and a cat at home. If you abandon them that long without providing for them, when you return you will have only a cat. Though all you will need to do for yourself is pack a bag with your swimming suit, tennis shorts, a robe and some toiletries, before you leave ask your neighbor to keep and feed the fish. You can leave extra provisions for the cat by exchanging large containers for her usual dainty dishes and filling each with dry food and water.

Uh-oh—You are driving from St. Olaf, Minnesota to Ft. Lauderdale, Florida with some friends for spring break? You will be gone ten days? This kind of trip requires a little more advance planning.

For yourself, gather together all the toiletries and personal care items you may need, from a hair dryer to bar soap. Heaven knows where you will end up sleeping—beaches don't provide amenities like candy mints on a bed pillow. Pack light, but make sure all your clothes are wash and wear, permanent press. Don't forget jeans and a light jacket; even in Florida, it is not always 80 degrees and sunny. If you have a camera, take it along. When you are middle-aged, you will appreciate the memories of this time when you were foot loose and fancy free. When you stop at the bank for funds, be sure to buy travelers' checks. Fifty dollar denominations are good. They are large enough that you won't have to use a check every time you want to buy a soda or a pack of gum, yet small enough that vendors won't be reluctant to accept them.

Travelers' Checks

It is not a good idea to take a trip without buying travelers' checks. Pickpockets and thieves are lured to vacation spots by thoughts of tourists carrying cash. As mentioned previously, I was robbed at gunpoint in the parking lot of a motel. I confess, the robber who got away with my purse did get my cash and all my credit cards. Yet my husband and I had some foresight: We had divided our travelers' checks and ready cash among ourselves and our luggage, so the robber did not get away with nearly as much as he might have. Nor was our trip ruined because our funds were all gone.

Still, that experience taught me something else. When traveling to strange cities, a woman should keep most of her funds and credit cards someplace other than in her wallet, which is carried in her shoulder bag. An inside jacket pocket or a body pouch is a good alternative. And men should not carry their wallets in their back pants pocket. Keep them in a front pants pocket. True, an armed robber like the one I had the misfortune to encounter would still be able to take it from you, but a pickpocket couldn't.

Homefront

As to the homefront, if you are going to be absent a week or so, you are going to need someone to tend to your apartment. If you have pets, ask a reliable neighbor or friend to come over daily while you are away to feed the carp and the cat, as well as to water your plants. Ask your neighbor to take in your mail and newspapers, too. An over-stuffed mailbox and newspapers piled up in front of your door are calling cards to potential burglars.

Before you leave, make a cursory check of your refrigerator. Remove any containers of leftover food—they will be fuzzy if you leave them until you return. Dump the dregs of milk from the carton, too, or it will reek odoriferously when it sours. When you set out in the morning, don't leave any food or dirty dishes on the kitchen counter or in the sink. If you do (and this is especially true if you live in an old building), roaches will be feasting during your absence. They won't leave when you return, either. Once they've discovered a buffet, they keep returning for seconds...and thirds...and fourths....

Disconnect appliances and fixtures before you leave on your trip. (Again, this is even more critical if you live in an old building that has equally old wiring.) Be sure your coffee maker, toaster, television set and other electrical items are unplugged—not your refrigerator. Though probably nothing would happen if you did not follow this tip, the old adage, "Better safe than sorry," is still true and for good reason.

European Vacation

What's this? Your father has presented you with a frequent flier airplane ticket to Europe? The chance of a lifetime? Three weeks in France, Italy and Spain? A trip of this magnitude and duration requires extensive planning to ensure your enjoyment and peace of mind.

Passport

First things first. If you are leaving the country, you must obtain a passport and possibly a visa. To get your passport, you must have your original birth certificate or a copy embossed with an official seal. Other variations of your birth certificate will not satisfy the government. If you or your mother no longer has your birth certificate, a copy can be obtained from the records office in the county where you were born. There is usually a small fee.

Next, you must have passport photos taken. A lot of photo studios offer "instant" passport photos. The cost is usually less than $10. Finally, you must pick up a passport application at your local U.S. post office. Complete it and return it to the post office with your photos, birth certificate, and fee. As of this writing, adult passports cost $65. If everything goes well, you can expect to receive your passport in about two weeks. If there's a snafu, however, it may take longer. Be sure to allow a longer amount of time, because you won't be able to board a transatlantic flight without a passport in your possession.

GETTING A PASSPORT

You will need:

- An application from a U.S. Post Office
- An official birth certificate
- A passport photograph
- To pay $65 when you submit the above at the Post Office

It takes two to four weeks to process a passport application

Visas

Some countries require visas. If you are planning to visit a country that requires a visa, your travel agent can assist you in obtaining one. You could also contact the nearest consulate for the country(ies) you plan to visit or ask for a copy of the pamphlet, "Visa Requirements of Foreign Governments" when applying for your passport.

Vaccinations

You may require vaccinations before visiting foreign countries. A travel agent or your local public health department can tell you which ones you may need. You will need proof of vaccinations if they are required where you are going, so be sure to get them.

Youth hostels

Before you do anything else, buy yourself a copy of *Let's Go Europe*. It is one of the best budget travel guides in publication, and it is updated annually. If you are planning to stay in youth hostels, contact the American headquarters of the International Youth Hostel Federation. [American Youth Hostels, Inc. P.O. Box 37613, Washington, D.C. 20013-7613—Phone # (202) 783-6161.] As an American traveler in Europe, you can't simply go to a youth hostel to spend the night. You must be a member of the organization. When you join (there is a small fee), you will be issued an identification card and a book listing all the hostels in Europe. You can also buy reservation postcards in advance. Plan your trip as precisely as you are able, and send in your reservations so that you will have a place to stay. Make sure you bring a sheet sack—blankets and pillows (and sometimes even breakfast) are provided by hostels, but you must have a sheet sack to sleep in.

Packing

Obviously, the lighter you pack, the easier it will be to travel. Plan on doing laundry a few times during your vacation. Don't try to bring enough clothes and underwear to last you the entire length of your trip without ever doing laundry or your back will break under the weight of your luggage. Be sure to take a portable alarm clock, a towel and soap if you will not be staying in classy hotels every night.

Language

If you don't speak the languages of any of the countries you will be visiting, invest in some English-foreign language phrase books or tapes. You can study them during the flight.

Medication

Don't bring medication if you don't absolutely need it. Drugs are a messy business you want to avoid. Even some medications available over-the-counter in Europe are controlled substances in the States. Things can turn sour quickly when you are going through customs if you are unsure about what you are allowed to take into a given country. Rule of thumb: If you need certain medications, be sure to carry them in their prescription bottles. Never transfer them to a pill box. If you buy over-the-counter pain relievers in Europe, throw them away before you board your return flight home.

Money

Of course, buy travelers' checks before flying off on your European vacation. At the international airport where you will be departing the States, cash $50 or $100 at one of the exchanges for your destination country's currency. As you travel from country to country in Europe, you will be able to cash American travelers' checks at banks and train station currency exchange booths.

Remember that buying and cashing travelers' checks costs money. When you originally purchase your travelers' checks at a bank, there will be a fee to the company issuing the checks. It will cost you $101 to purchase $100 worth of travelers' checks. If you use a check for a direct purchase, the vendor should take the check as if it were cash and give you exact change. But if you cash a check at a bank or currency exchange, there will be a fee for that service. So, when you change a $50 check for currency, you may receive only the equivalent of $48 American.

Safekeeping

Though there is a small expense in buying and cashing travelers' checks, again, don't consider carrying cash as a cost-saving alternative. Should you lose or be robbed of $1000 cash, it will be gone and your trip prematurely ended. But if the $1000 is in travelers' checks, they will be replaced.

As to the risk of loss or theft, there are certain things you simply can't afford to lose while traveling in Europe: your passport, your money, your return plane ticket. To help ensure these items' safety, buy a body pouch (available at most luggage stores). A flat canvas purse that you secure to your body beneath your clothes with a strap, it will hold your precious passport and reserve travelers' checks snugly out of sight. Don't keep anything in it you will need during the day; keep your spending money in your pocket. If you do need to retrieve something from the pouch, detour to a restroom so that no one sees your secret stash.

Keep a register listing the numbers of all your travelers' checks and places the checks were cashed somewhere other than where you carry the travelers' checks themselves. You will need this information if the checks must be replaced. Also, keep a photocopy of your passport somewhere else, too. You will need that information if your passport disappears.

Trains

Across the ocean, people travel by train much more frequently than we do in America. In fact, it's the most convenient way of moving from place to place. But simply because people ride the rails more often there than here, don't expect ticket prices to be exceptionally cheap. Depending on where you wish to go, tickets may, in fact, be quite expensive. Therefore, it might behoove you to purchase a Eurail Pass immediately upon arrival. There are various kinds: student, first class, some that are good for a month, some that are good for five rides during a two-week period. Decide which is the most economical for you.

Also, the train stations contain a wealth of information and services. You arrive in a new city and have no idea how to find your three-times-removed second cousin's house; or it is evening already and you have no idea where you might spend the night; or you are suddenly in Germany with nothing but French francs in your wallet. There are booths manned by people who can give you directions, find you accommodations in your price range, and even change your money from one currency to another.

At-home arrangements

As to your home, follow the tips mentioned for a shorter vacation, like the one to Ft. Lauderdale. But this time, leave your pets with a friend for the duration. Two, three, four weeks is too long to leave your animals alone, even if you could arrange for someone to come in each day and feed them. Again, ask a neighbor to water your plants, if you have any. But stop your newspaper delivery altogether and arrange for your mail to be held at your local post office.

Before you depart, give someone—perhaps a relative or a reliable friend—your planned itinerary and return date. It might be wise to leave some extra money in this person's care so that if you find yourself cash short while on vacation, you can phone and have your friend wire you your reserve funds. Also, leave a photocopy of your passport (not a picture of the cover) with this trustworthy soul. In case you lose your passport and the photocopy you have taken with you, the reserve photocopy will help you get your identification replaced.

Summary—Checklists

Travel requires planning and paying attention to details. Before you leave home for any length of time, it's wise to make a checklist. Here are some sample ones:

For a vacation of several days:

✔ Inform your family and place of employment.

- ✔ Pack appropriate clothing and necessary toiletries.
- ✔ Make arrangements for a neighbor to feed/walk any pets you may have and to water your plants.
- ✔ Ask this same neighbor to take in your newspapers and mail.
- ✔ Make sure this neighbor has a key to your place.
- ✔ Throw out any foods that will spoil during your absence.
- ✔ Make sure there are no dirty dishes lying around.
- ✔ Take out the garbage.
- ✔ Disconnect appliances such as televisions, toasters, lamps.
- ✔ Pick up travelers' checks for the bulk of the funds you intend taking with you on your trip.

For a lengthy vacation:

- ✔ Follow the list above, but instead of having a neighbor drop by to feed and water your pets and plants—
- ✔ Find someone willing to take in your pets, and possibly your plants, too, for the duration. An alternative is to board cats or dogs in a kennel.
- ✔ Stop at the post office and ask them to hold your mail there rather than delivering it to your home.
- ✔ Stop delivery of any newspapers for the length of your vacation.

For an overseas trip:

- ✔ Follow the complete listings above to ensure your home is secure, but also—
- ✔ Apply for a passport (and any needed visas) at least a month before your departure date.
- ✔ Get any vaccinations you may require.

- ✔ Consider having a trusted friend apartment-sit.
- ✔ Join the International Youth Hostel Association if you wish to take advantage of their inexpensive sleeping facilities.
- ✔ Buy a body pouch to carry documents and funds you can't afford to lose.
- ✔ Make two photocopies of your passport information, one to take with you, one to leave with a trusted friend or relative.
- ✔ Write out your itinerary and leave it with that friend.
- ✔ Buy travel, guide, and foreign phrase books that you will take with you.
- ✔ Be at the airport two hours in advance of your flight.

Bon voyage.

Recommended Reading

Harvard Student Agencies. *Let's Go (various titles): The Student Guide to (various titles)*. New York: St. Martins Press, Updated yearly.

———. *Fodor's* (various titles of travel guides). New York: Fodor's Travel Publications. Updated yearly.

FFF...

FOOD

The best thing about food is eating it. But there are a lot of things to do with food before it reaches your lips.

Food Shopping

Take buying it, for instance. I rather doubt you do much gardening or canning, so I assume you purchase food at grocery stores. Since you probably have paid quite a bit of hard cash for groceries, because of your experience you may think you know all there is to know about grocery shopping. You may be wrong.

Though the neighborhood deli, corner store, or gas station quick mart may be convenient for you, they are the most expensive places to shop. In some cases it may be impossible, but, if you can, shop at *warehouse grocery stores*. These places buy in such quantity they almost always undersell the competition.

Always write a list of what you need and intend to buy. Stick to that list. Only purchase additional items or select alternative items based on the specials you encounter.

Buy the 'lead' items advertised. If ground chuck is on sale forty cents less per pound than usual, even if you already have a pound or two in your freezer, buy some more. You will use it soon enough; take advantage of the sale price. If pears are on special for thirty-five cents a pound, even if you had no intention of buying pears this week, buy a few pounds. They are tasty, they are nourishing, and they will take the edge off your appetite for only a few cents each.

Buy house brands and generic products. They are cheaper than nationally advertised brands and are usually manufactured and packaged by those same companies that produce the nationally advertised products. Why pay extra for fancy labels and television ads?

Junk food isn't real food. Your mother made you eat your vegetables and roughage. Now that you are on your own, you will be inclined to consume only pizza and candy bars, corn chips and soft drinks. Your mother cared about your health. If you are smart, you will care about your health and continue to follow her advice. Junk food provides calories and virtually no nourishment. The result can be added weight, bad complexions, dull, limp hair, broken fingernails, lack of energy, numerous colds and low-grade infections. Doesn't sound pleasant, does it? A balanced diet of roasted and broiled meats, fresh, stir-fried or microwaved (not boiled) vegetables, pasta, potatoes, cheese, whole grain breads, leafy salads and an occasional egg or two will keep you healthy and looking great.

If you are not a great cook or your schedule is so hectic you hardly have time to cook, aim for one decent, well-balanced meal a day. If all else fails, splurge on "healthy" frozen dinners and entrees.

Coupons

Coupons mean cash savings. I know, coupon clipping is something old ladies spend a lot of time doing. But they do it because they live on limited incomes and coupons save them money. You live on a limited income, so it stands to reason coupons can save you money, too.

Nowadays, major grocery store chains run coupons every week in local newspapers (often on Wednesdays). If you already get a paper, it's not inconvenient to cut them out and take them along with your shopping list. Some grocery stores also send fliers filled with money-saving coupons through the mail. If they are delivered to your door, take advantage of them. Even a couple dollars saved every week adds up. Who couldn't use an extra hundred dollars annually?

When to Shop

Shop once a week. True, you may run out of milk or soda or bread, and then running down to the corner market to buy more is the reasonable thing to do. Also, you may be limited by the size of your refrigerator and freezer. But try to consider what meals you intend to prepare in the week ahead; shop only periodically for the foods and special ingredients you will need. If you don't stop at the store every day on your way home wondering, What am I in the mood for today? you will save yourself a great deal of money.

Never go grocery shopping when you are hungry. You will end up buying twice as much as you intended to. You will also buy things that appealed to you only because your stomach was growling, not because you want to prepare them later on during the week. You will buy the wrong things, too. Instead of a dozen jelly filled donuts, a loaf of bread and a quart of milk, you will buy three dozen donuts. Eat before you shop.

Food Storage

Food, especially fresh food, rots even in the refrigerator. Given enough time, hamburger turns brown, chicken starts to smell like rotten eggs, bad fish becomes so tearfully odoriferous it is impossible to describe. Vegetables like carrots and broccoli go limp, as do salad greens and celery. Badly wrapped cheese hardens into inedible bricks and milk curdles. In the freezer many foods can last months longer than they do in the refrigerator, but even they can "burn." That means they dry out and get hard, especially if they aren't wrapped well. Even ice cream becomes rubbery as the moisture is gradually sucked out.

Rule of thumb: Use fresh meats within a couple days of purchase. Use fresh vegetables within two weeks. Freeze fresh meats and vegies you don't intend to use immediately. When you take meat from the freezer, it is best to defrost it in the refrigerator rather than on the counter. Use defrosted meats within a few days of thawing. Use freshly thawed vegetables immediately. You may prepare the vegies directly from the freezer or thaw them first.

Fresh foods and cooked leftovers must be properly wrapped. If you stick a pound of hamburger into the refrigerator in its original store wrap but there's a hole in the wrap, the meat near the puncture will discolor and get hard. A half empty, open can of chili in the refrigerator will soon get hard and crusty. Leftover pork chops will dry out in record time as well. So make sure your foodstuffs are in air-tight, lidded containers or wrapped in plastic wrap or tin foil if you are keeping them in the refrigerator. In the freezer the same rule applies. However, plastic wrap loses its ability to cling when it gets cold, so in lieu of containers use tin foil or freezer wrap.

Some foods are rarely refrigerated and must be consumed quickly, especially during warm weather. Grapes, berries and bananas go bad very quickly and become hosts to swarms of tiny, annoying fruit flies. Fresh bread either dries out or spontaneously generates mold on its crust. Butter or margarine left out to improve its spreadability can go rancid very quickly in summer weather, if it doesn't melt into puddles first. And chips and crackers get soggy and stale if they are not kept in airtight containers.

About those fruits, there's nothing that can be done except to consume them quickly, so don't buy more than you can eat. Limp lettuce can be perked up by soaking it in very cold water for a few minutes. The shelf life of fresh bread can be increased by refrigerating it. In the freezer, it will last a long, long time. Though it is harder to spread, keep butter in the refrigerator, especially in the summer. Or buy tub margarine, which should be kept cold but still spreads easily. Sometimes, chips and crackers can be freshened by spreading them on a plate and popping them in the microwave for a minute—but not always.

STORAGE AND USAGE TIPS

- ✔ Use fresh meat within two days.
- ✔ Use refrigerated vegetables within two weeks.
- ✔ Properly wrap refrigerated foods to avoid hardening.
- ✔ Meat should be frozen in a good quality freeze wrap.
- ✔ Defrost meats in the refrigerator for a day or two, not on the kitchen counter top.
- ✔ Air-tight containers are best for food storage.
- ✔ Buy no more fresh fruit than you can consume in a week.
- ✔ Refrigerated bread lasts longer.
- ✔ Buy nutritional foods— you will have more energy, look better and be healthier.

Of course, there are some foods that seem to have an indefinite shelf life. Of those, there are some I would never recommend you buy, such as processed white bread, corn chips, snack cakes, and other junk foods. Others are designed to last, at least in the freezer, such as frozen vegetables, prepared meats, i.e. fish sticks, meat patties, TV dinners and entrees. Still other long-lasting foods Nature itself provides: apples, potatoes and onions.

So be careful what you buy, when you buy it, how much you buy, and where you buy it.

Cooking Food

Once you have your supplies and they are stored properly, you will still have to cook many foods in order to make them edible. There seem to be a million cookbooks on the market, so I won't give you recipes here. However, there are some basic things you should be aware of so that you don't have disasters in the kitchen:

Potatoes can be baked in a conventional oven at anywhere from 350 to 400 degrees for about an hour. They may be naked or wrapped in tin foil. Naked, the skins become a bit crispy; wrapped, they become soft. They may also be baked for a few minutes, naked, in a microwave oven. In any case, potatoes must be punctured or else they will explode. Simply stab them two or three times with a fork before putting them in any kind of oven.

Popcorn is popped in oil, not water. Pour a little oil in the bottom of a pot, heat it (not to the point of smoking), add the corn, cover with a lid, and shake the pot occasionally during the popping process. When your corn is done and you have put it in a bowl, you can melt your butter in the warm pan without returning it to the burner.

If you buy a rolled beef or pork roast, place it in the oven without removing the string. The string will not catch fire in the oven. I admit, living on my own at eighteen, I thought it would. I bought a beef roast to make a fancy dinner for my boyfriend and, noting the twine that bound up the meat and realizing it was made of fiber, I assumed it would catch fire in the oven so, I removed it. The roast unrolled during cooking and because it was flat, it cooked in a fraction of the time it should have. Instead of a fancy dinner, my guest and I could have resoled our shoes with what was to have been our main course. *Leave the string on.*

Pasta must be boiled in water. Not just spaghetti but egg noodles and elbow macaroni must be cooked in water that has already reached a bubbling boil before you add the pasta. This means that if you are preparing a casserole and the recipe says to "combine with egg noodles" an already prepared mixture of ground beef, onions and tomato sauce, you are not to add dry noodles directly from the bag. The recipe requires cooked noodles.

There is, of course, an exception. On the incredibly off chance you are making homemade soup, or if your casserole recipe anticipates the addition of pasta by first requiring an extra cup or two of water, you may then add dry noodles to the pot. The pasta will cook itself soft in the meat broth or absorb the extra water in your casserole concoction.

Put lids on pots in which you are simmering sauces and pans in which you are frying. Even on fairly low heat, these things bubble and sizzle, spattering everywhere—the stove, the walls, the floor. Lids will keep the spatters from going anywhere. If something threatens to boil over because a lid is in place, move the lid, placing it on the pot or pan slightly off center. This will allow steam to escape and prevent messy boilovers.

Preheating means just that: Turn the oven on to the temperature you desire at least ten minutes before putting any food in the oven to bake.

When you cook pasta or rice, strain it in a colander, then rinse it with warm water. This process stops the pasta from cooking further and getting pasty; it also washes excess starch off the rice. If you use cold rinse water, your spaghetti or rice will be cool and not too palatable.

Cooking Terms

Baking:	Cooking in a (conventional) oven.
Basting:	Moistening with gravy or liquid at intervals.
Boiling:	Cooking in boiling water. (212 degrees F. at sea level; so hot it is bubbling.)

Braising:	Searing in fat, then cooking, covered in a small amount of liquid or cooking by direct exposure to heat or flame.
Broiling:	Cooking by direct exposure to heat or flame.
Chopped:	Cut into small pieces.
Frying:	Cooking in hot fat or oil.
Grilling:	Same as broiling.
Marinating:	Allowing food to stand for some hours in a bowl containing a liquid mix of seasonings and flavorings.
Minced:	Cut into very tiny pieces, almost pulverized.
Roasting:	Cooking uncovered, without water, in oven.
Sautéing:	Cooking in small quantity of fat or butter.
Scoring:	Making slight cuts (scores) in outer surface.
Searing:	Browning rapidly at high temperature.
Simmering:	Cooking at a low temperature.
Steaming:	Cooking over boiling water or in a steamer.

Measurement Abbreviations

tsp. = teaspoon	Tbs. = tablespoon
C. = cup	pt. = pint
qt. = quart	gal. = gallon
# or lb. = pound	oz. = ounce

Measurement Conversions

3 tsp. = 1 Tbs.	2 Tbs. = 1 liquid oz.
16 Tbs. = 1 C.	2 C. = 1 pt.
2 pts. = 1 qt.	4 qts. = 1 qal.

All measurements should be made flat or level, not rounded in the measuring utensil.

Microwave Oven

If your microwave oven has high, medium, and low settings, follow this table:

Microwave Cooking Temperatures

HIGH	MEDIUM	LOW
Liquids	Pie crust	Yeast breads
Puddings	Poultry	Eggs
Sauces	Cakes	Cheese
Soups	Small roasts	Large pot roasts
Some meats	Defrost frozen *cooked* foods	Melting butter and chocolate
Fish		Defrost frozen *uncooked* foods
Vegetables		

In a microwave oven, DO NOT use:
Metal pots, pans or utensils
Tin or aluminum foil
Metal trimmed or metallic glazed dishware
Twist ties from plastic bags or wrappers
Clear, lightweight plastic, disposable beverage cups.

In a microwave oven, DO use:
Wax paper
Paper towels containing no nylon threads
Paper plates and cups
Heavy duty plastic bowls, cups and utensils
Heat resistant glass cups and baking dishes.
Standard ceramic and pottery dishware.

Summary

- ✔ Make a plan for grocery shopping before going.
- ✔ Don't grocery shop when you are hungry.

- ✔ Use coupons and shop for the specials.
- ✔ Proper storage and cooking prevents food waste.
- ✔ Learning to cook well takes practice.

Bon appetit

Recommended Reading

Bracken, Peg.*The Compleat I Hate to Cook Book.* San Diego: Harcourt, Brace Jovanovich, 1986

Elder, Joe. *Buy It Fresh, Keep It Fresh: The Complete A to Z Guide to Selecting and Storing Food.* New York: Ballantine, 1990.

Fitzgerald, Mollie. *On Campus Cookbook.* New York: Workman Publishing, 1984.

Hartwig, Daphne M. *Make Your Own Groceries.* New York: MacMillan, 1979.

Marlin, Alice T., et. al. *Shopping for a Better World: A Quick and Easy Guide to Socially Responsible Supermarket Shopping.* New York: Ballantine Books, 1992.

Patrick, Toni. *101 Ways to Make Ramen Noodles: Creative Cooking When You Can Only Afford Ten-for-One-Dollar Pasta.* Greeley, CO: C & G Publishing, Inc., 1993.

Wood, Jacquelin and Joelyn S. Gilchrist *The Campus Survival Cookbook.* New York: Quill, 1979.

GGG...

GIVING EMERGENCY AID

Sometimes accidents happen and you may find yourself the only one around or the first one on the scene. You will wish to perform First Aid or at least do the right thing until emergency medical personnel arrive or the injured party can be transported to the nearest hospital emergency room. People generally wish to help in such situations, but sometimes what they think is "helping" actually makes matters worse. This occurs because of a lack of training, knowledge, or a belief in "traditional" home remedies that are not, in fact, the correct procedure to follow. For instance, there is the old "butter on a burn" remedy. Actually, what can butter do but melt? The correct thing to do for a minor burn is to apply ice or cold water. And how about that old standby, forcing a person with a bloody nose to put her or his head back? What does that do except keep the blood from dripping on the carpeting—and force the bleeder to swallow blood which, in turn, may induce vomiting?

The following is a list of not uncommon medical problems or emergencies, and the procedures for you to follow if you are the first or only person on the scene to help. Remember, too—especially if the situation is serious enough to require professional intervention—not to panic. Also be sure to send for or telephone for professional help by calling 911 (if it is available in your city) or your community's rescue service through the police or fire department. If you don't have a 911 system in your town, keep the emergency assistance numbers permanently displayed on or near your telephone.

Back and Neck Injuries

If the person is breathing and is in no immediate danger, immobilize the victim exactly where she or he lies. Use anything handy, from purses to bowling bags, rolled blankets to bricks. Place them on either side of the head and next to the torso inside of the victim's arms.

If you must move a person whose back or neck is injured—perhaps because of a fire or other imminent danger—be sure not to twist or bend the injured person's back, neck or head. If possible, roll the person onto a board or blanket and drag it. If no board or blanket is handy, pull the patient away from the hazard either by the shoulders or the ankles.

Bleeding Injuries

To treat seriously bleeding wounds, apply pressure. Do this with fresh bandages or any clean clothing or towels. Put ice or cold water in the padding to help stop the bleeding and keep swelling down. If no clean cloth of any sort is available, use your hands. If bleeding doesn't stop, press harder. Remember, too, not to remove impaled objects and if the bandaging becomes blood-soaked, don't remove it, either. Just add another layer of padding on top of the soaked bandaging.

Another way to stop serious bleeding is the tourniquet. Use a tourniquet only on limbs, never the head, neck or torso. To make a tourniquet you need a strip of cloth at least two inches wide, like a scarf or a piece of sheet. The cloth must be long enough to encircle the limb at least three times. Place the tourniquet above the wound but not touching it. Tie a half-knot with the ends of the cloth and then put a strong, fairly straight stick on top of the knot. You can use anything from a ballpoint pen to a chopstick. Tie a double knot over the stick and twist the stick until the bleeding stops, but no tighter. Using the ends of the tourniquet cloth or another piece of fabric, tie the stick in place.

Previously I mentioned what not to do with nosebleeds. What you should do is have the bleeder lean forward (over a sink is nice), and pinch the nose just below the eyes with thumb and forefinger. Meanwhile, apply cold compresses (a wash cloth will do) around the nose area and/or the back of the bleeder's neck. If bleeding persists, pack the nostril(s) with a strip of clean gauze or cloth. Don't use absorbent cotton, which will stick. If the bleeding doesn't stop fairly quickly, seek medical attention.

Minor Cuts, Scrapes and Splinters

For minor cuts, scrapes and splinters always be sure to scrub the area clean with soap and warm water. If there is dirt or gravel embedded in the wound, use a soft toothbrush to get it out. Use an antibacterial solution to prevent infection. Cover with a bandage. Leaving wounds uncovered delays healing. Change the bandage if it becomes wet or soiled. If the wound involves a splinter, remove it with a needle and/or tweezers that have been sterilized by holding them over a flame.

Seizures

Some people have seizures, also called "fits" or convulsions. Don't try to restrain a person who is convulsing. Never try to put anything in a convulsing person's mouth, especially your fingers. Don't give the person anything to eat or drink until the episode is over, and never throw water in the person's face. What you can do is help the person lie down, especially if she or he feels the seizure coming on, as many epileptics may be able to do. Clear away furniture that could cause injury. Loosen tight clothing. After the seizure has passed, turn the person on her or his side to prevent choking on saliva or vomit.

Electric Shock

In cases of electric shock, be sure you don't expose yourself to the same injury. Not too many years ago, a couple of young boys in my home town died because the first touched a wire fence onto which a damaged electrical cable had fallen. When his brother grabbed him about the waist in an attempt to free him, they were both electrocuted. If you find a person in contact with a wire or electrical appliance, turn off the current before rendering assistance. If that is impossible, stand on a thick newspaper or rubber door mat and use a dry, non-metallic (preferably wooden) object to push the person off the wire or the wire off the person. Then cover the victim with a blanket or jacket until medical help arrives.

Fevers

Fevers can be scary, especially if they occur in small children. Traditionally, for reasons I'll never understand, people caring for fever victims bundled the patients up with excessive blankets and covers. *Don't* do that. Anyone who is sick with a virus or flu and running a fever should have no more than a sheet on, if they are comfortable. Drinking plenty of fluids, particularly water, is extremely helpful in treating fevers, as is the taking of aspirin or acetaminophen (Tylenol).[1]

If a person—especially a child—has a high, spiking fever (102 degrees or more), additional measures should be taken to bring it down. First try sponge baths. If that doesn't work, sit the patient in a tub of six to ten inches of tepid water so that most of the body is exposed to air. Afterward, dry the person rubbing briskly with a towel.

---

1 Giving aspirin to a child for any length of time can be dangerous. Children are susceptible to Reyes Syndrome, an often fatal condition associated with the taking of aspirin when suffering other childhood maladies.

With high fevers, in children or adults, be sure to consult a physician. Ask the physician about administering aspirin or other medication.

Exposure

Heatstroke symptoms include a temperature of 102 degrees or higher, hot, red skin but no sweating, confusion or unconsciousness, fainting and possibly convulsions. For someone suffering heatstroke, the best thing you can do is take them to a cool place, spray or sponge them off with cold water or alcohol, and call for emergency medical help.

The opposite of heatstroke is hypothermia; that is, exposure to cold outdoor temperatures or freezing water. Symptoms include the lack of shivering or "feeling cold," drowsiness and weakness, a low body temperature (below 90 degrees), pale, bluish or bright pink skin, slurred speech and unconsciousness. To treat, make the person warm. Remove any wet clothing and bundle the person in blankets or clothing. If nothing else is available, strip the victim and yourself, holding the person close to warm your own body heat. If the victim is conscious, administer warm, nonalcoholic drinks. Booze doesn't warm a cold person, despite the myth that it does.

Drowning

Drowning victims can often be saved despite a long period of not breathing. The colder the water they drowned in, the better their chances are. Once removed from the water, lay the victim on her or his back and turn the head sideways so water in the mouth can run out. If the victim isn't breathing, begin Cardiac Pulmonary Resuscitation (CPR). Reposition head so face is up, pinch the nostrils closed, and exhale four forceful breaths into the victim's mouth. Lift your own head to breathe and then repeat. If you are working on a small child or infant, give four gentle little puffs. Don't try to empty the lungs of water; you can't do it. Don't give up on someone who seems dead. Keep at it until emergency response personnel arrive.

Choking

When someone is choking on a piece of food, perform what is known as the Heimlich Maneuver. Stand behind the person, encircle her or his abdomen with your arms. Press the thumb side of one fist against the abdomen, halfway between the waist and the bottom of ribs. Grasp your fist with your other hand and give four quick, hard, inward and upward thrusts. If this is impossible because the victim is a very pregnant lady, make the thrusts inward against middle of breastbone. If you are choking, let those around you know. Don't discreetly hurry off to the restroom in a restaurant. Many have done this, and many have died. If you are alone you can perform the Heimlich Maneuver on yourself, or you can push against your abdomen by leaning over the back of a chair.

When a small child is choking the simplest thing to do is grab the child by the ankles, hang the child upside down, and whack the child firmly between the shoulder blades. The offending object should pop out.

Poisons

All poisons should not immediately be brought up via induced vomiting. If someone swallows a poisonous substance, read the warning label on the substance if at all possible and follow the instructions. Next, call the local Poison Control Center for assistance. If there's none in your area, call 911 or have the telephone operator put you through to a hospital emergency room.

In general, you don't want to induce vomiting if a person has swallowed a strong acid, alkali or petroleum-like product. You do wish to induce vomiting if they have swallowed medicines, plants, spoiled food, ink, perfume, suntan lotion, or rat poison.

Summary

- ✔ Take first aid, CPR and Heimlich Maneuver classes.
- ✔ Keep emergency numbers near your telephone.

- ✔ Don't panic in an emergency.
- ✔ Do what you can until professional emergency medical help is available.

Recommended Reading

Hill, Patricia B. (ed.) *Emergency Medical Procedures for the Home, Auto & Workplace*. New York: Prentice Hall, 1990.

Rosenberg, Steven N. *The Johnson & Johnson First Aid Book*. New York: Warner Books, Inc., 1985.

———. *The American Red Cross First Aid and Safety Handbook*. Boston: Little, Brown, 1992.

GGG...

HHH...

HOUSEKEEPING

Everybody hates housekeeping. Even Mrs. Cleaver, Beaver's mother, hated housekeeping. That's why she always wore a dress, high heels and pearls while she mopped the kitchen floor. She was always prepared—and hoping for a last minute invitation—to go shopping or out to lunch. Joan Rivers hates housekeeping because, she says, you finally get finished and then, six months later, you have to start in all over again. Yes, everybody hates housekeeping, especially *house cleaning*. But if you live anywhere except a cave, it has to be done with some regularity.

When you were a kid living at home, "cleaning" to you was straightening your room every month or so when your parents hollered at you, "Get in there and clean up that mess!" Your efforts probably took a total of ten minutes, during which you threw several weeks' worth of dirty clothes down the chute and dumped armfuls of sticky plates and glasses into the dishwasher. Next you pulled your bedspread up over rumpled sheets and, if there was any clutter still lying about on your bedroom floor, you pitched it into your closet, quickly closing the door after it before the debris could tumble back out into the room.

What you did was not really cleaning, it was "picking up." Your mother or your father or the cleaning lady cleaned. Now that you are on your own, those people are not going to clean your home. You have to do it yourself.

Your old style of cleaning—picking up—won't cut it. Picking up is something you will do frantically when unexpected visitors are knocking at your door. You will gather and stack newspapers, throw out old, smelly, carry-out pizza boxes, and pitch the three days' worth of clothes lying in your armchair into the hallway closet. Cleaning is different. Cleaning is removing dirt and it should be done fairly regularly, probably once a week.

Tools

How do you really clean? As with any project, begin by having the right tools. If you are going to work on an engine, you have to make sure you have the correct wrenches and screw drivers. If you are going to write a letter, you need paper and pen. It is the same with house-cleaning. Before you begin, assemble the right tools.

✔ A *mop, bucket, scrub brush* and *sponge* are basics. A sponge mop is the most universally efficient.

The bucket should be deep enough to hold a couple of gallons of water and large enough to accommodate the mop head.

✔ Clean rags.

Use your old clothes. Tee-shirts and dress shirts with the buttons removed make good dusting and cleaning rags. Cloth diapers also make good cleaning rags and you can usually find them at a discount department store. Frequently you will find bundles of clean rags for sale at a flea market.

✔ A *broom, dust pan*, and a *feather duster*.

✔ A *toilet bowl brush*.

- ✔ A *dust mop*.
- ✔ A *vacuum cleaner* for rugs or carpeting. Many canister vacuums have attachments that work for carpetless floors also.

A vacuum cleaner generally has a paper bag inside to collect the vacuumed dust, dirt, chips, popcorn, hair, etc. Check the bag on a regular basis before vacuuming and replace it when it is full. If it isn't replaced when full, the bag will tear and puffs of dirt will billow out every time you turn the vacuum cleaner on, not to mention the fact that the vacuum will not pick up the dirt.

When my elder moved out on his own, he got an old canister vacuum cleaner from someone. He always complained about what a piece of junk it was. Later, this son moved out of state, temporarily leaving behind in my basement a number of his possessions, including the vacuum cleaner. One day I had occasion to move this vacuum cleaner, and that gray, powdery, grimy dirt you can only find inside a vacuum cleaner came spilling out the nozzle. That's right. Dirt spilled out a nozzle on the end of a fifteen foot corrugated hose that was attached to the canister. When I took the machine apart, I found not only the bag inside the canister was filled with dirt, but the entire length of hose was filled as well.

Obviously neither my son nor the machine's previous owner had ever emptied the vacuum cleaner bag. That the vacuum picked up anything was incredible; that the motor had never given out was a miracle. But I was not going to pay to ship forty pounds of dirt and dust from Wisconsin to Louisiana.

My son was lucky. I have heard of vacuum cleaners that have exploded because the owners didn't change a full bag. Check it and change it when necessary.

Cleaning Products

Just as we use shampoo to wash our hair, liquid soap to wash our hands, and deodorant bars to wash our bodies, there are numerous products to clean specific inanimate objects. Consider purchasing a few of the following:

- ✔ Liquid lemon or pine cleaner to mop tile or linoleum floors
- ✔ Oil soap to wash wooden cupboards or floors
- ✔ Glass cleaner to do windows and mirrors
- ✔ Heavy duty, all-purpose spray cleaner to spot-clean appliances
- ✔ Cleanser or foaming bathroom spray for wash basins and tubs
- ✔ Liquid toilet bowl cleaner
- ✔ Spray furniture polish for dusting/polishing wood furniture

---

CAUTION

Mixing products can create deadly gases. For example, never mix an ammonia product with a chlorine product.

Or, you can use an all-purpose spray cleaner for just about everything from floors to sinks, and you can dust with only a rag. That will cut down on your purchase of cleaning products considerably, though you will still need a few specific cleaning products.

Where to Start

Once you have assembled your tools and cleaning products, where do you begin? At the bottom—Start with your floors. No matter how small, you probably have a kitchen with a tile or linoleum floor. First, remove chairs and other portable objects resting on the floor. Then sweep, scooping crumbs up into the dust pan, which you will then dump into the trash. Next, fill your pail 1/2-3/4 full with water and add a generous splash of liquid cleaner. (Or, spritz the all-purpose cleaner directly onto your floor.) Dunk your mop into the bucket of water, wring it out, and push/pull it back and forth across the floor. Be sure to catch the dirty suds that may accumulate; rinse and wring the mop frequently. If your floor is really dirty, you may have to forego the mop in favor of scrub brush and sponge. Do the same basic things, but on your hands and knees.

CAUTION

Beware of using cleaning solvents around water heaters, furnaces, stoves or any appliance or motor that is ignited by spark or operates with a flame. The fumes can combust, creating a virtual fireball.

The second linoleum or tiled floor you need to mop is the bathroom. Though bathrooms tend to be tiny, especially in apartments, that doesn't mean they are easy to clean. Heavy tressed females and balding males shed a lot of hair in bathrooms. Clean thoroughly and frequently around the toilet area. Sweep or vacuum before you begin mopping. If radiators, the toilet, and other objects make wielding a mop next to impossible, you will have to resort to scrubbing on your hands and knees. When you are finished mopping or scrubbing, dump the dirty wash water in the toilet, not a sink.

What's Next?

If some rooms in your home have wood floors, repeat the mopping process with oil soap or vinegar water instead of pine or all-purpose cleaner. They tend to eat through wax and varnish. Vacuum carpeting and large area rugs.

Once you have cleaned basically everything at your feet, you can move up to waist level. Dust can be temporarily eliminated by swabbing down flat surfaces such as table tops and lamp shades with a dry rag. Pick up things like lamps, candy dishes, and framed pictures. Dust the items in hand and the places they sit. If you wish, use furniture polish when dusting wooden objects to give them a protective shine.

Mirrors and glass require a spray glass cleaner and a clean rag. If your rag leaves lint or streaks behind, you can opt to use old newspapers instead. Newsprint doesn't leave lint nor does it smear printer's ink.

Lastly, use your all-purpose spray cleaner to do kitchen appliances and things made of vinyl, Formica and plastic.

Back in the bathroom again, scrub your sink with either cleanser, foaming tub and tile cleaner, or an all-purpose spray. Wipe off all toilet surfaces, but know that even the Tidy Bowl man can't keep up with the kind of dirt the toilet bowl takes on. Sprinkle cleanser or squirt a liquid bowl cleaner into the water. Then use a toilet bowl brush to scrub it clean, even under the rim. When you are done, flush and rinse the brush in the bowl's clean water.

Hair can be a real problem in the bathroom if it collects in sink and tub drains. To prevent clogs it is advisable to put a little drain cleaner in your bathroom and kitchen drains once a week.

Don't put drain cleaner in a garbage disposal drain.

There are harsh chemical drain cleaners, both liquid and granule, that you can purchase at grocery, discount and hardware stores. There are also natural bacterial powders that won't harm pipes. If you live in a really old building with very old plumbing, I strongly recommend the bacterial powders available through plumbing stores.

Final Stage (Higher Places)

Dust collects even on ceilings. It usually manifests itself as grimy tendrils of dirt that hang like streamers, or it knits together in corners like cobwebs. You can prevent this dirt from collecting by swiping at corners with a feather duster or rag, or you can wait till you notice it and then remove it. In either case, it's a good time to also dust those out-of-sight places, like the top of book shelves and door frames and even your refrigerator.

All the things involved in house-cleaning that I have just outlined probably sound like they would take an entire day to do. Not so. In an apartment, you could probably finish your cleaning in as little as thirty minutes. Besides, you don't have to do everything every cleaning day. If you have wood floors, you don't need to mop them weekly. Perhaps every other month or so is enough. In between mopping, simply swab them down with a dust mop. Shake a dirty dust mop clean outdoors, else all your work will be for naught. Dust web hunting doesn't have to be done weekly, either. Nor window cleaning. On the other hand, some things should be done quite often: vacuuming, dusting, sweeping and wiping off the stove, for instance. If you are not sure what needs to be done and when, play it by ear. Over time you will discover where and when dirt accumulates and how often it must be cleaned to keep your home both comfortable and presentable. Eventually, you will establish your own routine.

Years ago I read somewhere that a woman had invented a self-cleaning house. The floors were all pitched at slight angles and soapy water flooded them, followed by a clean rinse that drained away. Even the kitchen cupboards were sort of mini-dishwashers that self-cleaned the plates and glasses. I'm not sure how it worked exactly, or even if it did. But this lady's efforts were valiant. Most everyone would love a self-cleaning house. Except for the inventor, I know of no one who actually has one.

Some years ago, however, modern science at last offered the average homemaker a couple of technologically advanced appliances: the frost-free refrigerator and the self-cleaning oven. There's a good chance you grew up in a household that contained both. There's a good chance that now you don't have either.

Refrigerator Cleaning

So how do you clean, or more precisely defrost, a refrigerator that doesn't automatically perform that function on its own?

Begin by emptying it of all foodstuffs. Spread newspapers on the floor around the appliance. Put some drip pans—a couple of 9 x 13 inch cake pans will do—on a shelf below the freezer compartment. Then turn off or unplug the refrigerator.

Clean the refrigerator just before doing your grocery shopping when it is relatively empty.

Now you can simply leave it until the ice in the freezer melts away. Or you can help things along by boiling water in a couple of pots and then sticking the pots of steaming water into the freezer. The ice clinging to the inside walls of the freezer will soften so that you can chip it away. What do you use to chip at the ice? Everyone will advise you not to use a knife, but that's what everyone uses. Just be careful. If you poke a hole in the freezer wall, the Freon will escape. That is the stuff that makes a freezer cold.

Once they are removed, dump the ice chunks and the water into the sink. Dry both the freezer and refrigerator walls with toweling. Sponge clean the metal racks and vegetable and meat bins, if you have them. Turn the refrigerator back on again and replace the food you removed earlier.

Oven Cleaning

To clean a non-self-cleaning oven, first put newspaper on the floor and remove the oven racks. Spray commercial oven cleaner on the walls of the oven and soak according to manufacturer's directions. Though such products are less caustic today than they used to be, wear rubber gloves and ventilate the kitchen by opening windows. After the cleaner has had time to work, remove the foam and the dirt with a damp sponge. Finally, give the oven a clean water rinse and replace the racks.

Never use commercial oven cleaner on a self-cleaning oven.

Dish washing

You probably grew up with a dishwasher, but now find you must clean your dirty pots and plates by hand. How do you wash dishes without a machine or a maid to do them for you?

First, scrape any leftover food from the dishes and pans. If you have a garbage disposal, that's where these scraps go. If you don't, scrape them off your plates into either your bag-lined trash can or onto several sheets of old newspaper. Dump the dregs of any liquids left in mugs, glasses and pots down the sink drain. Don't pour grease or cooking oils into sink drains. Animal fats (grease from hamburger or chops) should be collected in an old can. The fats will harden when cooled, then throw the tin can away. Vegetable cooking oil such as corn or peanut can be reused after you have fried potatoes or chicken. Keep a plastic cooking oil bottle for "old" oil; don't combine used oil with fresh. Use the "old" oil for future frying. Don't use it as an additive in recipes, such as cake mixes.

Fill the sink or a plastic tub that fits into the sink with hot water. Add a squirt of liquid dish detergent while the tap water is still running. After the water is sudsy, start by washing the glasses first. Rinse them in clean, warm water. Dry glasses with a dish towel or set them upside down in a dish rack to air dry.

Wash the cleanest items first and the greasiest items last.

Wash silverware and utensils next followed by plates, platters and bowls. Again, these can be towel or air dried in a rack. After all your regular dishware, glasses, mugs and stainless are washed, wash your pots and pans. These may require more than a sponge or rag for clean up; you may have to scour them with a steel wool or Teflon pad. Baked or burnt on foods may require hours of soaking in soapy water before you can wash them clean. When they are clean, towel dry or stack to air dry.

Now let the water out of the sink. Though the drain must be open, make certain the drain strainer is in place to catch any pieces of food that ended up in the wash water. You don't want food particles to get into the drain, or eventually you will have a clog that will require the services of a plumber. Next, rinse the sink and scour with powder or liquid cleanser, or even an all-purpose spray cleaner. If you have used a dish rag and towel, be sure to hang them so that they can dry thoroughly. Damp cloths become musty at the very least; at the worst they serve as a spawning ground for bacteria. Be sure to wash them when you do the laundry.

Dump your trash or newspaper filled with food scrapings outside in the dumpster. When the dishes are dry, put them away.

Summary

- ✔ House cleaning is a dirty job that involves more than picking up the big stuff.
- ✔ Start with the right tools and cleaning products.
- ✔ Everything doesn't have to be cleaned each time.
- ✔ Over time work out your own routine of rotating the major jobs.

Recommended Reading

Aslett, Don. *Do I Dust Or Vacuum First.* New York: Signet, 1993.

Campbell, Jeff. *Speed Cleaning*. New York: Dell Publishing Co., 1987.

Campbell, Jeff. *Clutter Control: Putting Your Home on a Diet.*. New York: Dell Publishing Co., 1992.

Florman, Monte and Marjorie. *How to Clean Practically Anything*. Yonker, NY: Consumer Union, 1992.

III...

INSURANCE

Insurance is a subject you can learn a great deal about simply by speaking with the numerous agents who will contact you as soon as you get a telephone in your own name. People your age, just starting out in life, usually go one of two ways as far as insurance is concerned: Either they don't have any or they buy far more than they need. In fact you don't need much coverage, but you probably need some.

Vehicle Insurance

If you own a car or a motorcycle, you need insurance coverage. Even if the state you live in doesn't require vehicle insurance by law, you risk losing everything if you drive uninsured. You may have nothing of any consequence or value right now, but some day you will—if only a decent paying job—and should you be involved in a traffic accident for which you are found liable, your future financial life could be ruined. It isn't worth the risk.

It is unnecessary to carry the maximum limits of liability. A rusty old car worth less than $750 doesn't require collision insurance. Liability will cover accident damages. If an insured driver hits you, her or his carrier will pay for damages to your car. However, if you "kiss a tree" on your own, you have to pay for the repairs. As your vehicle is of minimal value, it is more cost effective to risk paying for repairs or buying another used car if it is totaled than to pay collision insurance premiums.

If you have a good used or brand new car, you need to carry liability, comprehensive (for damages caused by vandalism, acts of nature, property loss and medical) and collision insurance. Don't, however, allow yourself to be talked into low or no deductibles. Though a $100 deductible seems standard these days, $500 is more reasonable. If you have a fender-bender, you will have to pay for minor repairs costing less than the deductible. But over the course of a year or two, providing you don't have frequent accidents, you will save more than $500 in premium payments.

Life Insurance

There are two kinds of life insurance, whole and term. At this point in your young life, you don't need either.

Whole life is basically a savings plan. You pay premiums for twenty, thirty, even forty years, and if you don't die first you can collect a sizable amount of money when the policy matures. Ideally, this money will augment your retirement income. Because you are probably scraping by, adding the heavy expense of whole life premiums to your limited monthly budget would be foolish. Anyway, IRA and 401K plans are more flexible and usually provide a better return on your investment than whole life.

Term insurance normally offers a very high benefit for low premiums while you are young. Term insurance often provides excellent protection and security for young families with children. It isn't a good investment for young persons just starting out on their independent lives. If you have no spouse, house, or dependent children, you don't need it.

In a nutshell, you don't need any kind of life insurance—unless you are alone in the world or your parents, too, live on a tight budget. In either of those cases you might want to buy a small policy to cover the cost of your burial in the event of your death. Otherwise, forget life insurance for now.

Homeowner's Insurance

Even if you don't own a house or condo, you may need homeowner's insurance.

Homeowner's insurance for the apartment-dweller is sometimes called renter's insurance. Renter's insurance covers only the apartment's contents. If you are nineteen years old, a college student living off campus in a fifth floor walkup, and all your clothes and furniture were purchased at Goodwill, then you don't need renter's insurance. However, if among the threadbare furniture you have an expensive stereo system, a computer, an electric guitar and sound equipment worth several thousand dollars, then you may want to have your belongings insured. Ratty old tenements are the first kind of buildings to burn down in large cities. They are also some of the easiest to burgle. As renter's insurance is usually quite inexpensive, it may well be worth the cost.

If you have new furnishings you couldn't resist buying on time payment plans, seriously consider having them insured. Should they be stolen or destroyed, your payments will continue even though the furniture is gone.

Health/Dental Insurance

This is the kind of insurance it has always been said no one can afford and no one can afford to do without. Now, many people must do without. Health insurance is very expensive, especially if taken out independently. Even someone with a healthy income would find the monthly payments a strain. If you are living on a shoe string budget, health plan premiums are beyond your means.

Many employers offer group health insurance to permanent employees. Even if you have to pay part of your monthly premium through payroll deductions, the cost is a fraction of an independent health policy premium. If you attend college, your parents' health insurance will cover you until you are at least twenty-three years old or cease to be a full-time student.

On the outside chance you are unable to obtain health and dental insurance through work or family, and you are a college student, you should be able to get student insurance through the school. Should that avenue not be available to you either, pray you don't get seriously ill. If you do get sick, take advantage of student services' medical clinics, or other free clinics and government-subsidized medical facilities offering healthcare to those without insurance or the financial ability to pay the customary fees.

Summary

- ✔ If you own a vehicle, you need some type of auto insurance.
- ✔ Life insurance can wait.
- ✔ Depending on the value of your belongings, renter's insurance may make sense for you.
- ✔ Health insurance is a definite plus; if it's not available to you through your parents or work, frequent free clinics until you can afford health insurance.

Recommended Reading

Dacey, Norman F. *What's Wrong With Your Life Insurance.* New York: MacMillan Publishing Co., 1989.

Pond, Jonathan D. *1001 Ways to Cut Your Expenses.* New York: Dell Publishing, 1992.

Sloane, Leonard. *Book of Personal Finance.* New York: Times Books, 1992.

JJJ...

JOB HUNTING

If you are out on your own and unless you inherited money or you grew up working as a juvenile television star, you have probably already held a job. But you may lose it. Or you may only now be forced to find employment because you are suddenly and unexpectedly on your own. You may have finished your schooling and are presently seeking to secure employment in your chosen career field. In any case, job-hunting can be a frantic, demoralizing endeavor, so here are a few hints to make things a little easier.

If you are still going to school, you are probably looking for a "blow off" job, the kind of low-paying, rotten-hours job no one would want to do for a lifetime. You assume—and in many cases, rightly so—that these are the only jobs available to you because you have no particular skills or experience, and school takes up a lot of your time. However, if you are able to be just a little discriminating, you could make a "blow off" job into something more substantial. Do this by searching for a job that can provide you with more than the small source of income you need to survive.

Instead of applying for absolutely anything from parking garage attendant to drugstore soda jockey, look for positions that may be in the career field for which you are ultimately aiming.

If you want to become a paramedic, try for a job with an ambulance service. If your dream is to one day be a manager of an exclusive resort hotel, apply for hotel jobs, anything from maid to room service to restaurant waiter. If you are in veterinary school, obviously a position as a receptionist at an animal hospital or as a cage cleaner at an animal shelter would provide training not available in books. The same holds true for the future buyer who works as a salesclerk in a department store.

Employers prefer recent graduates who have more than classes to their credit. Some hands-on experience is helpful. Even simply having worked in the environment of your career choice would be a plus when applying for your first full-time career position.

Perhaps, though, you have no idea what you want to be when you "really grow up." Maybe you are taking general classes in college now and have not yet chosen a major. You may be out of high school or college and not sure what direction to take. You need a job to pay the bills. Look at positions, then, that may include some variety, teach you new skills or offer advancement.

If you take a position in the service department of a car dealership where your primary duties are to greet customers and tag their keys, perhaps you will learn to use a computer. If you find yourself a file clerk at a small construction company, perhaps you will be expected to assist when the secretary is out by answering phones and typing letters. You may even get the opportunity to learn to use a word processor. Or you could be hired as a busboy at a local pizzeria, but eventually work your way up to night manager.

Such part-time or temporary jobs give you a taste of the working life. They will help you to learn as much about what you don't want to do as they will help you decide what you do want to do. Along the way, you will learn new skills that will enable you to move on to better paying jobs elsewhere or will groom you for promotion to a better-paying position within the company.

For example, one of my high school-aged sons took a job as a "carry out" for a building supply store. In that position, his responsibilities were to collect shopping carts from the parking lot and to help people carry heavy, ungainly purchases from the store to their vehicles. Eventually he was promoted to a department where he learned how to do everything from stocking shelves to driving a fork-lift. If he went on to college locally, he could probably stay with this company and continue to earn promotions and raises while still working part-time. If he were interested in earning a business degree, he would probably have the option of making this store and the corporation of which it is a part, his adult livelihood. If he didn't choose to do this, the experience he has in retailing and the skills he's learned such as fork-lift driving will enable him to get a better than-minimum-wage job elsewhere.

My other son's first job was as a busboy. At another restaurant he was trained as a cook. But he always thought waiters made the most money, so eventually he got a waitering position at a casual Italian restaurant. Later, when he took a year off from college to work full-time, he applied for work at a fancy, four-star French restaurant. Though he didn't have much experience as a waiter and had absolutely no experience in fine dining, the fancy restaurant hired him on probation and taught him "table service" (making salads and specialty coffees and Cherries Jubilee at the diners' tables) and sent him to classes on the finer points of champagne and liqueurs. He moved from establishment to establishment and the skills learned along the way helped him move up and on. Though he has no intention of becoming a career waiter, he has experience that should prevent him from working only minimum wage jobs throughout his long college career.

Make the best of the worst kind of jobs. In the long run, they may help you to land a good job. Adopt a positive attitude and present yourself in the best possible light. Even if a lousy job is just that, a lousy job, you need that job now to pay your bills. Make yourself stand out from the crowd so you land that job.

Dressing For an Interview

Beware of projecting a "blow off" demeanor that announces to a prospective employer you are not very impressed with the available position and would never be interested in it if you could find anything else to do. Make sure you are neatly dressed when you show up for an interview or just to fill out an application. You might get an interview even though you hadn't planned on one.

Dress conservatively and a cut or two above what you would wear to class or to a friend's B.Y.O. party. This means a sport coat, dress shirt and a tie for a young man and a skirt or dress with pantyhose for a young woman. If you are auditioning for a heavy metal rock band or applying as a sales person at a boardwalk, open-air art gallery, you can dress to express your personal creativity. But in most businesses, a conservative standard of dress is required. Even if the employees seem to have no dress code or are required to wear uniforms, when you apply for any job be well-kempt and well-dressed. I have personally seen young men rejected for mail room and "gofer" positions because they arrived for their interviews dressed in jeans, tennis shoes and tee-shirts. I have also seen otherwise qualified young women rejected for receptionist positions because their ragged fingernails were painted with chipped, black polish, or because their blonde hair sported two inches of black roots.

When you arrive for an interview, get there a few minutes early. Don't smoke or chew gum. Smile and be friendly, but don't presume. That means, don't take a chair unless it is offered. And always go to your interviews alone. Never bring a friend along, even to wait in the reception area and especially if she or he has also applied for a job at the same establishment.

Resumé

If you have completed your education and are now seeking to land that first, full-time career position, there are numerous books available with step-by-step instructions and advice on everything from networking to dressing for success to interviewing.

When looking for part-time, low-paying employment, your first contact with the potential employer is usually at your interview. But when seeking higher paying, full-time positions that constitute a career move, your first contact is through your resumé. Your resumé must be letter-perfect with no typos, spelling, grammatical or punctuation errors.

I can't emphasize this enough. But I am not advising you spend a lot of money to have a professional business writer compose your resumé, or that you have it duplicated at great expense by a professional printer, or that you include a little photo of yourself in the upper corner of the first page. It is fine if you type your resumé yourself and simply photostat additional copies. *Just make certain there are no mistakes.*

My husband is the personnel manager for a large, national corporation. Again and again he marvels at how seemingly illiterate even multi-degreed individuals appear to be. They use the word *lead* when they mean *led*; they don't know the difference between *its* and *it's*; they use non-words such as *irregardless* or *orientated.* Our personal favorite was a man who, in his resumé, described his "entreé level position." He was a computer programmer, not a chef.

No matter how skilled or experienced you are in your chosen field, it will reflect very badly on you if you can't communicate well. Should your resumé contain either glaring errors or typos, those you have sent it to may wonder at your basic intelligence. How did you get through school without knowing the basics of your own language? Or they may simply feel you are not thorough or detail-oriented enough to handle a position of any responsibility. In either case, you will have blown your chance to land a position with the company before you have even reached the interviewing stage.

Read your resumé over and over, proofing it for errors. Give it to several other people to look over before you prepare a final version for submission.

Self-employment

If you would rather not work for others and you would prefer a potentially unlimited income, self-employment is another option.

During high school you may have had a part-time job at the local fix-it shop. You are good with tools, and it seems you can get almost any sort of engine working again. Your family and neighbors know you know how to fix things. They bring their broken lawnmowers and toasters to your house and ask you to work on them when you have time. You do, and you charge a few dollars for your labor and the parts.

Why not have business cards printed, and advertise in the local paper? You could end up with so much work you will not need any other part-time employment.

If you are a musician who is now a music major in college, why not give lessons? People can send their children to various music stores in your city for lessons. But how many people offer in-home lessons? That could be your gimmick. You will go to the students rather than having them come to you. Again, have business cards printed and advertise in local papers, on grocery store bulletin boards, at music stores, and even in schools.

There are lots of different ways to become self-employed. Some of them require initial investments, some don't. Some are risky, some are less so. But depending on your circumstances and your financial resources and needs, becoming self-employed may be a real option for you to consider.

Summary

- ✔ Finding a job is like a job and takes a lot of thought and action.
- ✔ Even when looking for part-time work to get you through school, look for jobs in your field of interest.
- ✔ Always dress appropriately and be well-groomed, even when filling-out applications. You may be unexpectedly asked to speak with someone in personnel.
- ✔ Especially for career-type positions you will need a resumé. It should include the necessary job-related information, be grammatically correct and well written. Consult a couple of books on job hunting and resumé writing.
- ✔ Consider self-employment as an alternative to working for others. Be creative. You may have a marketable skill you have taken for granted.

Recommended Reading

Bolles, Richard N. *What Color Is Your Parachute?* Berkeley, CA: Ten Speed Press, 1993.

Crowe, Patrick H. and Gregory D. *Money Grubbing, A Student's Guide to Part-time Jobs & Self-run Business.* Chicago, IL: Chicago Review Press, —.

Yate, Martin J. *Knock' em Dead: With the Very Best Resumés.* Holbrook, MA: Bob Adams Inc., 1988.

Yate, Martin J. *Knock' em Dead: With Great Answers to Tough Interview Questions.* Holbrook, MA: Bob Adams Inc., 1987.

KKK...

KEEPING YOUR MONEY SAFE—SAVINGS AND INVESTMENTS

There are two type of savings: saving for retirement and non-retirement savings. Let's start with non-retirement savings and investing, since this is what you will need first.

Non-retirement savings may have many purposes but basically it can be broken down into two categories. One category is short-term (two months to two years) and would mainly be used for things such as vacations, appliances, furniture, stereo equipment, car downpayment and expensive sports equipment. The other category is longer term and might be for a downpayment on a house, to start your own business, and unforeseen emergencies such as periods of unemployment, extended illness not covered by sick leave, and major car repairs.

Whatever the purpose of your regular savings plan, you will want it to be fairly liquid. The most common forms this savings may take are passbook savings, mutual funds, and certificates of deposit.

Liquidity refers to how easily you can turn your savings or investments into spendable cash.

LIQUIDITY

Some examples of liquidity from the greatest to the least are:

- Cash-on-hand
- Checking Accounts
- Passbook Savings
- Mutual Funds
- Certificates of Deposit
- Individual Retirement Accounts and 401Ks
- Property, such as a car or house

Passbook Savings Accounts

Traditionally, most middle class Americans put their extra dollars into passbook savings accounts at banks, savings and loans, or credit unions. As a child, you may have been given your own passbook account into which you put birthday and special occasion money, and perhaps a percentage of your allowance or part-time job earnings. You, like your parents, squirreled away savings that earned 4% or 5% interest. Maybe you were saving for a new bike or an old car; maybe your parents were saving for a house, a vacation, or their old age. In any case, your savings were safe—insured by the FDIC or FSLIC—and though they didn't reap a great profit, they did earn a satisfactory amount of interest that increased your holdings by an acceptable margin.

There is still nothing wrong with passbook savings accounts. If nothing else, by keeping certain moneys separate from your checking account funds, you won't be tempted to spend them until you need them. When you do need them they are there and they are liquid, meaning you can withdraw them at any time without penalty. But if you are really trying to save a sizable amount, putting money into passbook savings isn't the way to make your fortune. Consider the following example:

To save $ 2,000 in the next five years you must save each month:

$29.28 in a passbook account at 5% interest	OR	$33.33 ($1/week more) in the "cookie jar"

To save $10,000 in the next five years you must save each month:

$146.40 in a passbook account at 5% interest	OR	$166.60 ($5/week more) in the "cookie jar"

True, it would cost you less out-of-pocket to accumulate a specific amount if you deposited funds in an interest-bearing account, but not a great deal more because passbook savings don't pay high interest. In this example, I'm using a rate of 5%, but as I write, most passbook savings accounts are paying around 4%. If you use such a savings account in an attempt to build a sizable nest egg, you will find it close to impossible.

You should also note that the interest rate quoted you isn't the rate your savings will actually be growing at. For example, if the earnings rate is 4.0%, you are in a 15% income tax bracket, and inflation is running 3.0%, realized earnings value on a $1000 savings balance will be as follows:

Passbook savings balance	$1,000.00
At 4.0% interest you earn in one year	40.00
Less federal tax on earnings @ 15%	6.00
Actual earnings after tax is	34.00
Your actual earnings rate is 3.4%	

In addition to the deterioration of the earnings rate, the value of your savings will decrease over time due to inflation. That is why it is important to maximize your earnings without unduly risking your savings.

Mutual Funds

Any individual may participate in a mutual fund. If, in addition to saving for your future retirement, you wish to increase your earnings through investments, you may wish to invest in a mutual fund on your own. Some funds allow you to join with as little as $250. Mutual fund shares can be purchased in easy monthly installments—as your extra cash allows—and often through an automatic monthly withdrawal arranged by your bank.

A mutual fund is usually made up of stocks (sometimes bonds) of several companies. Investing in a portfolio of stocks managed by professionals will generally be safer than investing in individual stocks through a stockbroker. Also the pooling of several stocks under one fund allows many small investors to purchase stock in the fund for a smaller initial investment than if they were buying individual stocks through a stock broker.

If you are willing to devote a little time to researching the various mutual funds, this may be the best earnings on your savings.

WHAT IS A NO-LOAD VERSUS A LOAD FUND?

Every mutual fund must charge its investors for managing and administering the fund. However, some funds are cheaper than others. Invest in a no-load fund. A no-load mutual fund will charge you only a percentage (as low as 1%) of the value of your account usually once a year. This is a lot better deal than a load fund, which charges for each transaction you make.

Certificates of Deposit (CD)

Certificates of Deposit (CD) are another popular savings technique. Instead of depositing varying amounts and withdrawing them as needed, in this sort of savings plan a person purchases a certificate that is redeemable after a specified period of time. A CD's price is specific: $1,000, $2,500, $5,000, or whatever amount you choose. The length of time the money must remain "locked into" the certificate is specific: for example, six months, a year or two years. This means that you can't buy a CD with whatever spare cash you have. You must have the required amount. Also, the funds are not liquid. You can't get your cash back until the designated time period has elapsed without paying a penalty. If you cash in a CD before its maturity date, you will lose the interest for the time remaining, and you will pay an additional penalty, usually one month's interest. However, by buying a certificate for a specified amount and holding onto it for the designated time period, the owner of a CD was traditionally paid much higher interest rates than a passbook savings account paid—anywhere from 8% to 15%.

But things have changed. The economy fluctuates, banking practices are regulated and deregulated, old laws are discarded and new laws written. Presently, CDs are paying about the same 3-4% interest as passbook savings, so they are no longer the bargain they once were. In fact, they have become a limiting investment because, unlike passbook savings, the funds are not liquid and available for use without penalty. Still, the economy and interest rates are sure to change as they have in the past, and one day Certificates of Deposit may again be a profitable and sound savings opportunity.

Retirement Savings

You are young. You would like to be well off in your middle years and comfortably set when you retire. But you are young, and being your parents' or grandparents' age seems impossible to imagine, so you are certainly not concerned about it. Unfortunately, as every year passes, the next one seems to speed by more quickly. It is inevitable that your hair will thin or turn gray and those lean, hard muscles will go soft. There's nothing anyone can do except die young to keep from earning the title, "Senior Citizen." The period from Thanksgiving to Christmas is an eternity to a child but the period between the birth of your own child and her or his high school graduation will fly by in a blur. Even though your own old age is literally decades away, it is a good idea to start planning for it as soon as possible in your youth.

Old age isn't death and each generation of workers seems to be retiring at an earlier age with many, many more years of active life ahead. Yet there is speculation about the future of the Social Security system. Acknowledging the possibility that Social Security may be of less value in the future, everyone should try to increase her or his net worth and build a nest egg of funds to live on or to supplement Social Security in retirement.

I know there is a real possibility that all you can afford now is to pay rent and buy food. You are scraping for tuition payments and you may not have health insurance. Every penny is needed in order to get by month-to-month. This will change. You will graduate from school and embark on a career or you will get a better job than the one you have now. As your employment situation improves, so will your spendable income. You can choose to raise your standard of living in direct proportion to the increase in your earnings or you can choose to live on less than you earn and invest in your future.

Individual Retirement Accounts (IRAs)

With an IRA, you contribute money you have already paid tax on but you may then qualify to take all or part of that contribution as a tax deduction. The amount you are allowed to use as a tax deduction is your tax-deferred contribution to the plan.

You can open an IRA at just about any financial institution. To qualify you simply must be a wage earning worker, self employed or the spouse of a wage earner or self-employed worker, providing you open a joint IRA and are under the age of 70 1/2. Contributions made to an IRA may be tax deductible up to a $2000 limit per year for single individuals. If you contribute tax deductible amounts to an IRA, you will not be able to use the 1040EZ tax form to take the deduction. You must use a 1040A or 1040 form.

The IRA tax deduction may be reduced or eliminated if you are covered by another retirement plan. Your IRS tax form instruction book has a worksheet to determine what the deductibility is.

You can't withdraw the money before you reach the age of 59 1/2 without paying a penalty, currently 10% of the amount withdrawn, in addition to paying withholding tax on the withdrawal.

401K Programs

A 401K plan is another type of tax-deferred investment plan. This plan, however, is only available through an employer who offers the plan. Unlike a traditional pension plan that is completely funded by the employer, a 401K plan offers employees the chance to contribute pre-tax dollars directly to the plan.

Many companies also match contributions to the employee's 401K account, usually as a percentage of dollar the employee contributes up to a certain percent of the employee's gross pay. For example, a company may match each pre-tax dollar the employee contributes with 50 cents but only up to 6% of the employee's gross salary.

Employee's yearly gross earnings	$20,000
Employee contributes 8.0%	$ 1,600
Employer's matching contributions	600
Total annual contributions to the 401K	$ 2,200

Your contributions into a 401K are made with pre-tax dollars. This money is deducted by your employer directly from your gross pay before being taxed. This money is taxed only when you begin to withdraw it for retirement between the ages of 59 1/2 and 70 1/2.

The money you contribute and any amount contributed by your employer on your behalf are invested by your employer to earn a profit and grow. Beginning in 1992, companies with 401K plans must offer at least three investment choices to employees in the plan. Company contributions to your 401K don't totally belong to you until you are 100% vested in these contributions. Usually a company will establish a minimum length of time you must be employed before the company contribution is considered a permanent part of your account. When you are 100% vested in the plan, you will be able to move all the account funds including company contributions to another retirement fund should you leave the company.

If your company offers a 401K plan, don't hesitate to sign-up for it. It would be difficult to beat the earnings and tax savings of a 401K retirement plan, especially if the company matches some of your contributions.

ROLLOVER

The money you contribute to a 401K plan belongs to you. If you should leave that company for any reason, you will be able to transfer that money ("rollover") to a 401K at your new company or to a retirement fund at a financial institution. There are no penalties or taxes to pay when you rollover the account because it remains intact and you are not using the money.

Keogh and Self-employed Plan (SEP)

These retirement plans are for the self-employed or those who work for the self-employed. I only mention them so you will know of their existence. I recommend you seek professional guidance to find out more about them.

Summary

- ✔ The time to start saving and investing is now or at least as soon as possible.
- ✔ Your most immediate savings need will be nonretirement savings. Don't put money into a retirement fund with the expectation of using it for other things before retirement. You will pay penalties and taxes on withdrawals from an IRA or 401K account before age 59 1/2.

- ✔ Take the time to investigate many savings options, chose the one that is best for you at the time, and invest whatever you can on a regular basis.
- ✔ Keep track of how your investments are doing. A good investment today may not be a good investment tomorrow.

Recommended Reading

Krefetz, Gerald. *All About Saving*. New York:. John Wiley & Sons, 1987.

Sloane, Leonard. *Book of Personal Finance*. New York: Times Books, 1992.

LLL...

LAUNDRY

You now know there's a washer and dryer or at least a rock and a stream between the dirty clothes that pile up on your bedroom floor and the freshly folded and ironed ones in your closet and dresser drawers. There used to be a mother figure who went with the washer and dryer, but she's gone now. These days there are just you and a local laundromat.

When you go to the laundromat, you have to bring things other than a duffel bag full of your dirty laundry. The supplies you need are:

- ✔ Change
- ✔ Detergent
- ✔ Fabric softener
- ✔ Bleach
- ✔ Stain remover
- ✔ Measuring cup
- ✔ Laundry basket
- ✔ If you can reasonably manage them, hangers

Bring a pocketful of change because the change machines in a laundromat are guaranteed not to work, at least not on the days you do laundry. Bring detergent and additives because those available in vending machines at the laundromat come in small packages worth their weight in gold. Buying them at the warehouse grocery store or at a discount drug store is much, much more economical.

Sorting

Sorting should be done according to fabric type and colors. Generally the more delicate the fabric and the darker the color, the cooler the water temperature should be and the less likely any bleach should be used. Remember the life of any fabric is shortened when bleached frequently and washed in the hottest water. Always go with the gentlest treatment that will do the job.

CLOTH TYPE	WATER TEMPERATURE	BLEACH
Permanent press		
Light	warm-hot	mild
Dark	warm	none
White cottons	hot	regular
Delicate (light & dark)	cold	none

It is a good idea to read the manufacturer's washing instructions on the label inside the garment. Because the manufacturer wants to avoid complaints, the label gives you good tips for garment care.

Wash your most delicate fabrics and the wash-but-don't-machine-dry load at home by hand in a sink. If you have any items that are both delicate (shrinkable) and colorful (they "bleed" in water), you will have to wash them separately by hand and hang them to dry. If combined even in a cold water wash load, they will stain the other items in the wash. To dry these kinds of clothes, throw them over the showercurtain rod or invest in handy flat-dry screens or collapsible drying racks.

Foldable drying racks for hand washables can be purchased at a discount department store.

Stain Removal

This is best done before you go to the laundromat, but if you have not, now is the time to run a prewash stain stick along the inside of soiled shirt collars or wherever you have noticeable dirt or spots on your clothes. I recommend using a stick rather than a liquid because sticks are more portable, less messy, and if you use one on a spot or stain as soon as you spill (even days before your laundry day), it will help keep the stain from setting without ruining the cloth.

Washing Machine

Set the washer for the right water temperature and put the correct change in the coin slot. As the water starts filling the tub, add your detergent. A cup of soap is enough, even for the big machines. However, it is best to read the instructions on the detergent package. Use more and you will create too many suds—enough, possibly, to spill out of the machine. If you are not Tom Hanks and you are not making a movie, you don't want that to happen. Next, add the appropriate pile of clothes.

Never pour liquid bleach directly onto clothes—bleach weakens fabrics. You can pour color-safe bleach directly onto clothes, but color-safe bleach isn't really bleach and whether or not it whitens whites is debatable.

Dryers

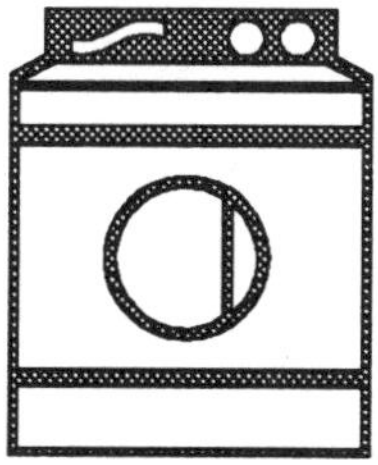

Once you have put the clothes into soap and water in each machine, close the lids, sit down, and read a book. When your laundry is done, put those items that can be dried into a dryer. You can usually combine whites and permanent press in a commercial dryer. Dryer time is sold in increments: ten minutes for 25 cents, for example. Instead of pumping a dollar's worth of quarters into a dryer and assuming they will take forty minutes to dry, put in enough for ten minutes only, then check. If your permanent press is dry but your towels are not, remove the permanent press items immediately and give the towels another round or two. By the way, if you didn't put liquid fabric softener into your wash during the rinse cycle, you may wish to throw one or two fabric softener sheets into the dryer with your damp clothes. The sheets are more convenient, especially at a laundromat. Fabric softener, either liquid or sheets, prevents annoying static cling and does make fabrics feel soft.

A note about home dryers. More than a couple of people I have spoken to recalled having problems with the first dryer they purchased as part of a washer-dryer set. It seems that after several months, their dryers stopped working. Even after an hour or two of spinning, their clothes came out damp. One woman actually wrote a complaint to Sears and Roebuck, suggesting that she might need a new felt pad.

Automatic dryers do *not* contain any sort of felt pad. What they have are lint traps. If you never empty the trap, the lint will eventually become so thick and packed together it may very well resemble a length of felt fabric. It will also keep the dryer from heating to desired temperatures and prevent the clothes inside from drying properly. Always empty the lint trap before using the dryer.

BACK TO YOUR LAUNDRY

Wool sweaters and cotton knit shirts should not be dried in a machine. When you remove them from the washer, hang them or put them in a plastic bag to be hung or flat dried later at home.

If you have a car or the laundromat is within a block or two of your home, folding and hanging your laundry as soon as it comes out of the dryer will save you a lot of ironing. If this is impractical, quickly toss your dry things into one duffel or plastic garbage bag, and any damp hang-or flat-dry items into another. Then hurry home. There, allow your sweaters and/or cotton knits to dry, and fold the remaining laundry.

Ironing

Even today many articles of clothing require ironing after laundering. It's impossible to describe ironing, so if you don't know how to iron ask someone to show you. Just remember to iron clothes on appropriate heat settings: delicate, permanent press, cotton. An iron's temperature doesn't adjust instantaneously. If you have been ironing cottons on a very high heat and turn the setting down to delicate to touch up a silk blouse, remember to wait several minutes until the iron cools. Otherwise the still very hot iron will scorch or melt your delicate blouse or shirt.

Non-washables

Other items can't be washed at all: Wool-blend trousers, raw silk blouses, tailored jackets and blazers, for example, must be dry cleaned.

Read the care tags on your clothing and follow the directions.

Summary

- ✔ Bring your own soap, whitener and fabric softener to the laundromat. It is much cheaper than buying them there.
- ✔ Just in case the change machine is not working, bring your own change.
- ✔ Sort your clothes by fabric type and colors.
- ✔ Wash very delicate items or hand-washable wool sweaters at home.
- ✔ Make it a habit to read the manufacturer's washing instructions for your garments. Also read the instructions for using your detergent, whitener and fabric softener.

Recommended Reading

Williams, E. Todd. *The First Men's Guide to Ironing.* New York: St. Martins Press, 1992.

Frandsen, Betty Rae. *Where's Mom Now That I Need Her: Surviving Away From Home.* Sandy, Utah, 1983.

MMM...

MAIL

There are two kinds of change of address cards you can pick up from your local post office: a large card that should be sent to your former post office (the one in your old zip code area), and smaller cards that should be sent to places which regularly send you mail.

First fill out the large card, which will ask for information about your former address, your new address, and your moving date. Sign it, address it to your old post office, and drop it in the mail. This card requires no postage and should alert your old post office to divert mail to your new address. The post office will do this for about six months.

Second, fill out the smaller cards with the same information. Mail these cards, which require postage, to people and places that regularly send you mail, organizations of which you are a member, and magazines to which you subscribe. The post office will not forward your mail indefinitely, so advise the sources of your mail of your new address.

If you receive mail, open it. When you were a kid, even in high school, you rarely received important mail. Now you do.

Window envelopes are seldom sweepstakes mailings. More often they are bills that must be paid within a specific time period. What appears to be junk mail could actually be important. Be sure to open and at least glance at all your mail before you opt to throw it away.

If you ever receive a product in the mail that you didn't order, you don't have to pay for it. Even if the accompanying information states that the product is yours for a free trial and if you are not interested in buying the product you may just return it, you don't have to send the product back. It might be in your best interest to inform the company you are not interested in buying their products, but you can keep what was sent to you unsolicited.

Chain letters are illegal. Whether they are for recipes, cash or promise misfortune and death if you break the chain, they are illegal. Don't waste your time with them or worry over them. Ignore them or file a complaint with your local post office.

Summary

- ✔ When you move, notify your old post office with a change of address card you can get at any post office.
- ✔ Also notify others who regularly send you mail that you have moved. Obtain these change of address cards from the post office.
- ✔ You don't have to pay for products you receive in the mail but didn't order.
- ✔ Ignore chain letters and don't participate in them. They are illegal.

NNN...

NEIGHBORS

When you move out on your own and have no roommates, neighbors are all you have. Cultivate them.

Whether or not you have ever lived in a large city, you have certainly heard stories about New York where there are frequent incidents of someone being in real trouble—getting murdered or raped—and though the neighbors heard the commotion, no one did anything to help. The reason this sort of thing happens is that even though people may live crowded together in huge apartment complexes, they often live in isolation. Most people don't know their neighbors on sight, let alone by name. They keep to themselves, hoping to avoid conflicts and trouble. Unfortunately, when serious trouble happens, there is no one willing to get involved and assist the victim.

Getting Acquainted

If people make an effort to know their neighbors, a sense of responsibility and protectiveness develops among them. For example, my elder once lived in low-rent area most people considered a less-than-desirable neighborhood. But he knew nearly everyone in his building, and they knew him. One night he returned home very, very late and he made more than a little noise locking up his motorcycle. Immediately lights came on and curtains opened. The people whose apartments faced the street all looked out to see if somebody was messing with his bike. My son waved and when they saw it was their neighbor, they waved in turn and went back to bed. This is a perfect example of neighbors looking out for each other.

You don't have to force close friendships with your neighbors. You may have little in common with most of them. But fast friendships can sometimes develop. This same son moved half-way across the country to a large city in which he knew no one. When he took an apartment, he met his upstairs neighbors immediately. They were all the same age and got along famously. During the week my son waited in an empty apartment for his furniture to arrive (including the vacuum cleaner with forty pounds of dirt inside it), he actually lived with his neighbors, both eating and sleeping with them. They became his first friends in a strange, new city.

Even if you don't become true friends with your neighbors, it is good sense to be friendly with them. If, in a short conversation at the mail boxes, a neighbor mentions he is going out of town for a few days, offer to collect his mail or bring in his newspapers. Should you be forced to borrow a stick of margarine from the lady next door, be sure you reimburse her quickly with not just a replacement stick, but a full pound box. These same neighbors will probably, in the future, be willing to water your plants if you go out of town, or to take delivery of packages that may arrive while you are at work.

A Little Goodwill

Besides overt efforts to be friendly, simply be considerate.

- ✔ Don't practice your trumpet or drums at eleven o'clock at night.
- ✔ Don't blast your stereo at eleven o'clock in the morning, knowing your next door neighbor, who works third shift, is probably asleep.

- ✔ Don't let your cat jump from your balcony to the balcony next door, where it likes to use your neighbor's flower box as a litter box.
- ✔ Don't forget to advise your neighbors beforehand if you are going to have a party that will run long and a little loud. Perhaps you could invite them to come or ask them to call you if they are in any way disturbed.

A little goodwill goes a long way toward keeping the peace. It also engenders a sense of community, and those within a community—even an apartment building—tend to look out for each other. If everyone looks out for each other, there is less chance an intruder can cause you bodily harm or property damage to your possessions.

Summary

Cultivate your neighbors—

- ✔ Get to know them.
- ✔ Let them get to know you.
- ✔ Be considerate and extend yourself a little when the occasion arises.
- ✔ Look out for each other.

N N N . . .

OOO...

ORGANIZATION

The key to being a successful adult is organization. In this crazy hectic world of ours if a person isn't organized, she or he is doomed. You know this already, for even in high school and college you had (or still have) to juggle classes and school work with football practice, dance lessons, a part-time job and ski club outings while maintaining some kind of social life and allowing time to eat and sleep.

Things get worse as you get older because with age most people take on more responsibilities. You will probably have a full-time job as well as other responsibilities to yourself and others. These responsibilities might include scheduling doctor appointments, children's music lessons, athletic and other school and club activities. This is in addition to unexpected emergencies and routine necessities such as cooking, cleaning and laundering.

As someone somewhere once said, "It ain't easy." But it can be done, and most people realize organization is the key to successfully managing a modern life. It is why there are so many books, seminars and service firms peddling tips on how to get organized.

You don't have to spend a lot of money to learn how to become organized. You only need to utilize three basic tools: *lists*, *calendars* and *containers*.

Lists

If you can remember everything you have to do and you know where you can get your hands on anything you will ever need, you will be organized—and on top of your life. Okay, it sounds nuts, but it is true.

Unless you have a perfect memory, you will probably forget one of the dozen things you have to do today, a few of the hundred things you have to do this week, several of the million (or so it seems) things you have to do this month. To help you remember, write everything down. This isn't a novel concept. Back in grade school your teachers told you to keep an assignment notebook. If you didn't misplace the assignment notebook, it was a great tool. It helped you to hand in your assignments on time and contributed to your earning good grades.

Do the same thing now. What sort of things would you write on *your* list? Anything and everything. Write down what needs doing and when it needs doing, and then put the list someplace visible. The refrigerator is a good place. Invest in some cheap decorative magnets and hang your list of things to do on your refrigerator door. That way, even if you forget where you put it, sooner or later you are going to go to the refrigerator for a snack and you will see it posted there.

To Do List

~~*Pay bills—Tues*~~
Pickup dry-cleaning—Thurs
~~*Buy kitty litter*~~
~~*Get Mom's gift & card Mon pm.*~~
Mail Moms gift—Wed

Call home Sat.

Get extra key made
Susan—date 8 Sat
Oil change appt.—Sat 9am
Make shopping list Wed
Grocery shop—Thur

Of course, the list will not help you if you don't use it. Make a habit of reading it, deleting and adding to it. Perhaps a good time might be every morning when you go to grab your wake-up orange juice. If you tie a string to a pencil and tape it to the refrigerator door, you will be really organized. Then when you glance at your list every day, you can cross out what you have already done and add any new things.

Calendars

Another organizational tool you need is a calendar. I prefer the big wall calendars that display an entire month at a time with each day in a nice-sized box for jotting things down. I can see at a glance everything I have coming up in the weeks ahead. My husband prefers a large appointment book. He doesn't use it just for appointments, but as a combination journal and life planner. He keeps it with him at all times. Of course, you could even use one of those little pocket calendars the card stores give away free. They are handy and the price is right.

When you get your first organizational calendar, you may have to call around to get the information you need. Be sure to put down all the information you have for the entire year, not just the upcoming month. In order for the calendar to work for you, you have to get a new one every year in late December or early January. Once you have completed a year using an organizational calendar, you can transfer a lot of information from the old to the new. Birthdays and anniversaries of your friends and family are not going to change.

Some of the important dates are not personal. Holidays, for instance, will already be highlighted in the calendar when you buy it. But what other kind of dates will you need to remember? Your new girlfriend's birthday, perhaps. The night two months hence for which you have concert tickets. Your rotating days off from work. The time you have scheduled for a vacation trip out west. Your dad's retirement party. Your nephew's first communion.

If you use a wall calendar, be sure it is hung somewhere you will see it daily. If you use any other kind of calendar, the sort that is bound like a book, be sure you glance ahead at the days

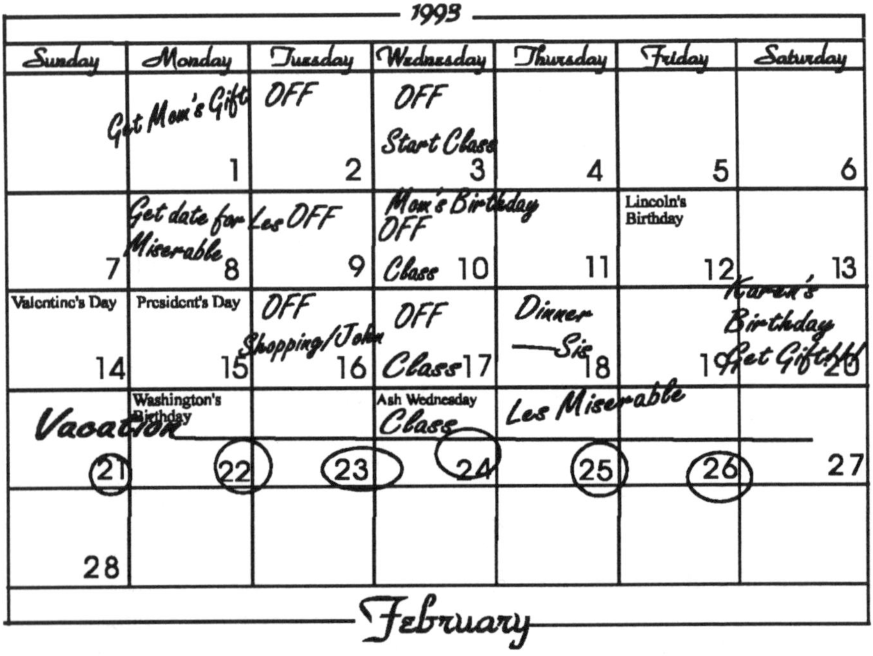

and weeks in the immediate future. For example:

✍ Your sister calls and invites you to dinner the following Tuesday. You glance at the calendar and discover Tuesday is, indeed, one of your scheduled days off from work. But you also see noted there that you are committed to going shopping in "the big city" with your best friend. You tell your sister Tuesday isn't a good day, but you are available Thursday. Could you come to dinner then instead? She says yes, so you jot down "Dinner—Sis" on that particular Thursday's date line. And as this is in the very near future, you will probably want to add it to the refrigerator list, too.

Both lists and calendars are simple, almost common sense ideas. They are systems that work and provide the underpinnings for overall organization.

Containers

Think of a well-stocked kitchen: Ice cubes and ice cream are kept in the freezer, coffee is in the canister marked coffee, flour in the canister marked flour. Why would anyone put something in the wrong place? If the sugar was in the canister marked tea, then you would have to remember that the tea was in the bread box. Too confusing.

As the well-stocked kitchen goes, so too should go your life. Things should be kept in suitable, well-marked containers. Otherwise...

☹ You can't find your car keys and you are late for school. You are in a panic, ripping apart the sofa cushions and groping through the dust bunnies under your bed. You miss your class before you finally find your keys in the jeans you put in the dirty laundry basket,.

☹ Your VCR is eating tapes, but you bought it only two months ago. You know it is under full warranty for 90 days, but where is that receipt? Where is that warranty? If you don't find them, you will have to shoulder the complete cost of repair or replacement. And you can't find them.

How do you avoid such disasters? There's another old adage, "A place for everything, and everything in its place." Words to live by. All it takes is some containers.

They can be very simple containers.

☺ Keep an empty candy dish or small bowl on the bookcase or TV in your front room. Every time you come through the door, drop your keys into it. That way you will always know where they are and you will never find yourself hunting for them on your way out.

☺ Household tools should be kept together. Someone invented tool boxes for that very purpose, but a spare drawer in the kitchen will do. When you use them, return them to their proper place so that you will know where they are when you need them again.

☺ What about receipts and statements you will need for taxes? If, in the course of the year, you don't accumulate all that many, use an envelope—anywhere from a regular or business-sized #10 to a large manila. Mark it "Tax Stuff" and keep it somewhere logical, like the middle drawer of your desk. Then when you have some documentation you need to keep, shove it right into that envelope. You don't need to file it or to keep the receipts in any kind of order. Just keep them together in a handy, well-marked container.

☺ The same holds true for receipts for products and their warranties. Get another envelope or a shoe box and write "Product Receipts" on it. That way if something is defective long before its time, you will have the required proof of sale that will guarantee you free replacement or discounted repairs.

☺ Other things you should store in containers range from important documentation such as deeds, titles and birth certificates to photographs to hobby equipment to out-of-season clothes. Deeds and other important documents should be kept in a metal fire-resistant lock box. In lieu of an album, photographs can go in a shoe box. School memorabilia as well as hobby equipment can also be stored in appropriately sized boxes. Those bulky sweaters you don't have room to keep in your drawers during the dog days of summer should go in boxes, too—clearly marked—or in transparent, plastic storage containers. This way, when the first unseasonable cold snap hits in September, you will know right where to go to retrieve your cable-knit cardigan.

☺ Remember to mark all the containers and not to switch the contents without noting it on the outside of the box, envelope or can. It is more than a surprise to find your envelope marked "Tax Stuff" containing old concert ticket stubs or your sweater box completely empty.

Fire resistant metal lock box	Deeds Car title Birth certificates
Shoe box	Photographs Hobby equipment School memorabilia
Clear plastic bags or storage boxes	Cable knit sweater Sports outfit/equipment

You can use these basic tools to set up simple systems to make you organized. If you haven't yet, now is the time to start. Use these tricks and tactics to help you run your life smoothly before you are responsible for anyone else besides yourself. Starting small, you will be able to handle the multitude of really big responsibilities that will come your way over time.

Summary

Three tools will help you to start getting organized.

- ✔ List to remind you of *what* needs to be done.
- ✔ Calendars so you will know *when* important events will take place.
- ✔ Containers to help you locate *where* important papers and things are.

Recommended Reading

Fanning, Tony. *Get It All Done and Still Be Human: A Personal Time-Management Workshop*. Menlo Park, CA: Kali House, 1990.

Melchior, Debra. *Organize Your Home: How to Store Clothing, Kitchen Items, Tools and Other Clutter Efficiently and With No Wasted Space*. Holbrook, MA: Bob Adam, Inc., 1992.

PPP...

PESTS

If you live in an old house or apartment building, chances are you may be plagued by unwelcome house guests—the multi-legged or furry varieties. If you have not been visited yet but wish to spare yourself unwanted company, the best thing to do is be clean and neat.

General Guidelines

In particular, don't leave foodstuffs lying about the kitchen or under your bed or the living room furniture, the way you did as a youngster. This includes empty soft drink cans on the counter, bread on the table and cereal bowls in the sink with a few flakes swimming around in a bit of milk at the bottom. If you do, you may come home to find little gray mice tunneling through your loaf of honeyed wheat and big, brown roaches poised on the edge of your Crispy-Crackleys bowl. Other precautions include taking out the trash daily, especially after you have prepared a meal and dropped both food packaging and scraps into the bin. Also, rinse out soda cans and bottles before disposing of them.

If you see no signs of mice, rats, roaches, ants, centipedes or silverfish but you know other apartments are infested, you may fear an eventual invasion. To prevent one, periodically spray your home with a commercial insecticide, but be sure to read the directions for cautions concerning pets and humans.

Rodents

If you already have mice, be sure to store your bread and donuts in the refrigerator or a secure metal bin and keep flour, sugar, and any other dry edibles, in air-tight, impenetrable containers. Metal bins, old coffee cans, glass apothecary and large pickle or mayonnaise jars are best. Plastic containers, whether Tupperware or old sherbet containers, are not as effective because rodents can gnaw through them.

DON'T ENCOURAGE PESTS

Keep foodstuffs stored in a safe place.
Rinse dishes or wash and put away immediately after use.
Rinse out soda cans and bottles before putting in the trash or recycling bin.
Take the trash out daily.

Buy the kind of mice or rat poison that forces the rodents to seek the outdoors before they die. Traps are all right, but you must dispose of the carcasses. Besides, they only catch or kill one rodent at a time. Poison is much more efficient, especially if you set it out where you have discovered mouse droppings. You know mice frequent the area already and are likely to feed on the poison you provide. Get a cat, ideally an older cat that was taught by its mother to kill for food, but any kitten will do. It will still catch and kill mice, but it will play them to death over long periods of time rather than killing them swiftly. It may also present you with its kill as if it were a special gift. (Yuch!)

A WORD ABOUT KITTENS AND CATS

If you live in an apartment, get either an older cat that has never been allowed outside or a kitten you will never allow outside. If cats don't know the outside world, they don't long for it and are completely content indoors. Be prepared to have the cat spayed, though. Unneutered males spray to mark their territories, and fertile females cry continuously when they are in heat.

Crawly Things

If you are infested with ants, throw out everything they are into. For a while you may have to keep powdered mixes for pancakes, muffins and cakes in the refrigerator. Spray with an ant-killing pesticide or buy little "ant motels" and leave them where the ants are sure to get into the poison and die. Silver-fish and centipedes like dampness. You will often find them crawling up out of a tub drain. If you live near a river or in a generally damp, humid climate, there is little you can do except spray or air condition your apartment. Air conditioning may be a luxury you can't afford, so kill the centipedes on sight and make sure your towels and other clothing are completely dry before you fold them and tuck them away. Otherwise, the silver-fish will make their way into your clean linens and clothes.

Grandfather of Crawly Things—The Cockroach

Cockroaches are another matter. They've survived and multiplied since before the Ice Age, and should there be a nuclear war, they alone will survive the fallout. You will have little luck in thwarting them once they arrive in your home, unless you are ever-vigilant.

Cockroaches live in cracks and crevices, behind cupboards and walls. They like the damp, but especially they like the dark. They usually only come out en masse during the night to look for a little action. So don't pad barefoot into your bathroom in the wee hours of the night. God knows what you will be stepping on if you have roaches for roommates. Instead, flip on the bathroom light while you are still in the hall. The little devils will probably scurry back under the baseboards as fast as their hairy little legs can carry them. Since they like dampness, never leap into your tub or shower stall without first looking, either. Rattle your shower curtain; flash your ceiling light.

To keep them under control, store foodstuffs securely and keep the garbage pail free of edibles. If you have no rodents to contend with and you have not yet invested in canisters to store your flour and sugar, put those staples, still in the bags they came in, into other, larger, plastic bags. Twist-tie the bags closed to keep out the roaches and other insects.

Spray with industrial strength, roach-killing pesticides. Buy "roach motels" and strategically place them about your home. Mix equal parts of corn meal, sugar and boric acid. Set this natural, homemade poison out in (clean) bottle caps.

I have been told there is a particular kind of lizard that is a natural roach predator. Apparently these reptiles are becoming quite popular in New York. You may want to investigate this lead and buy yourself a lizard instead of a cat for a pet.

No matter what you do, keep it up. When you have not seen a cockroach for a few weeks, that doesn't mean you can stop spraying or buying fresh "roach motels." Be careful, though, if you have a house pet, that any poisons you set about the apartment are out of reach of your animal. And when you spray, be very careful nothing you will consume, cook in, or eat off of gets contaminated. Pesticides aren't good for people, either.

Summary

To minimize pests in your home:

- ✔ Keep foodstuffs cleaned up and put away.
- ✔ Take the trash out frequently, even daily.
- ✔ Clean-up dishes and utensils right away after using.
- ✔ Use bug sprays, poisons and traps when necessary—always use caution.
- ✔ Consider a cat for a pet to discourage visiting rodents.

Recommended Reading

Graff, Debra. *Pest Control You Can Live With: Safe and Effective Ways to Get Rid of Common Household Pests.* Sterling, VA: Earth Stewardship Press, 1990.

Hamm, James G. *The Handbook of Pest Control.* New York: Fell, 1982.

Stein, Dan. *Dan's Practical Guide to Least Toxic Home Pest Control.* Eugene, OR: Hulogosi, 1991.

PPP...

QQQ...

QUALITY AND PRICE

There is an old saying, "You get what you pay for." Some might argue with me, but my advice to you is: Buy cheap.

My advice is applicable to almost anything you may buy. For example, generic products cost much less than name brands but are often produced by the name brand manufacturers. Since you are getting the same contents, isn't it foolish to pay more for a fancy label?

SALE
30% OFF

Furnishings

Suppose you have just landed your first, full-time job and are moving up to a nicer apartment than the one you had in college. Though you don't wish to furnish it with your Salvation Army castoffs, don't purchase handcrafted French Provincial. What you buy today doesn't have to be handed down to your grandchildren. It simply has to be functional and fairly comfortable. Besides, if you presently favor sleek leather couches and glass tables, a decade from now you may well be into Victorian mahogany. Also, if there is any chance you may wed within the next ten years, your furnishings will have to combine with your spouse's. Odds are they won't mix well and you will discard nearly everything to start over together. Even then you will probably, eventually, have children. Trust me:

Coffee tables with little teeth marks in them and unmentionably stained arm chairs are nothing you will wish to hang on to during your middle age. Thus, I strongly recommend not putting yourself in debt by buying heirloom quality furnishings today.

Electronic Stuff

Leaving the subject of furniture behind for a moment, bear in mind also that what is costly, state-of-the-art electronics equipment today will be inexpensive and nearly obsolete not too many years from now. Though people are still buying pricey, wide-screen TVs, shortly we will be introduced to high density screens that will make our current televisions as inferior as our black and white sets became with the introduction of color. Let's not forget what happened with calculators. When they were first put on the market they were fairly large and very costly. Now they can often fit in the palm of your hand and are given away free in boxes of cereal.

Just a few years ago I purchased the first home word processor that was available. Within six months the manufacturer came out with several upgraded models and each one's capacity was about double that of its predecessor. More annoying, the price of each model dropped nearly $100. And did you know that in the beginning, VCRs went for $1200 to $1600 a piece? Would you pay that for one today? Of course you wouldn't. It is for this reason I strongly advise you to purchase modest stereo, computer and other electronic equipment at equally modest prices. Sure, you need it to do what you want it to do (don't buy a tape player when you want a VCR that records as well), but forego a lot of gadgets and special features that add to the purchase price. Really—If there's no remote control with your TV, so what? If getting out of your chair to change channels means a saving of a hundred or more dollars, I'd say the exercise is well worth the savings, wouldn't you?

Selling Schemes

When you do go shopping, beware of upselling attempts. For instance, your television dies and in the morning's newspaper you spot a local store's ad for a small model at a great price. Knowing you can dip into your meager savings to purchase a set for that price without closing your bank account, you head out to the store. As soon as a salesperson shows you the sale model, she or he takes you aside and explains, confidentially, that the company which manufacturers the television is notorious for using bad sound boxes. Eventually, the salesperson says, the audio will be laced with static. However, for only $$$ dollars more you could buy a major brand TV set with a quality speaker, one that will never fail you.

This, my friend, is called upselling. The store advertises a product at a very low price, possibly below cost, as a lead item. The intent is to get people in the store. The sales person's job is to sell people more expensive items so they can earn a higher commission.

Don't fall for it. I've been buying lead items all my life, much to the chagrin of the salespeople who have assisted me, and these items have served me well. Of course, if the advertised item is obviously inferior, don't waste your money. And beware of a store that pushes shoddy merchandise even as lead items. Don't buy anything from such a store.

Buying Used

An alternative to buying new is buying used (preowned) merchandise, mainly through classified newspaper ads, but also at resale stores, garage, rummage, and estate sales.

I wish to emphasize here that I am not advising you to be cheap, only reasonable. If you buy bargain-priced items that are worn or inferior and which must repeatedly be repaired or replaced, this would be an unwise and costly endeavor. But it would be even more costly and just as foolish to spend top dollar, which you can hardly afford at this time in your life, for possessions you will no longer want in a few short years.

Summary

- ✔ Make purchase selections based on the lowest price and reasonable quality.
- ✔ Don't spend a lot of money on items you may not want or need in a few years.
- ✔ Keep in mind that when hi-tech electronics products, such as VCRs, calculators, CDs, and personal computers first came out, the prices were very high compared to today's prices for the same item.
- ✔ When a new electronic gadget comes on the market, wait to see if it will be a stable, useful product and watch the price go down.
- ✔ Shop secondhand stores, garage sales, flea markets and auctions for bargain goods.

RRR...

ROOMMATES

The odds are that after you leave your parents' home you will, at some point, live with a roommate. Roommates can be a blessing or a curse. In most cases, they are simply a matter of necessity.

On television, in movies and in novels, roommates nearly always seem to get along famously, even when small misunderstandings result in minor arguments or humorous confusion. There always seem to be at least one roommate who can cook and another who is fastidious and picks up after everyone else. Therefore, all the roomers are well-fed and their apartment is clean, and there is never any doubt that the rent will be paid in full and on schedule.

In reality, living with roommates is never such an ideal situation. Most often, roommates share living space and expenses because, though one person would love the privacy, she or he can't handle all the expenses. People rarely become roommates because they are old, dear friends who wish to live together. More often they become roommates because one or more answered a newspaper ad offering accommodations for a fractional share of the rent. Therefore, many roomers don't know each other before they begin living together, and personalities, habits and schedules often conflict. Even when roommates have known each other previously, living in close quarters together sometimes creates annoyances and conflicts where otherwise there would be none.

Selecting a Roommate

Not that having roommates is all bad. They are better than neighbors because they are usually aware, on a daily basis, of whether you are alive or dead. To a degree they replace family members as someone you can count on in emergencies. Of course, roommates are great because they usually enable you to live in convenient, comfortable accommodations none of you could afford individually. But when you become or take on a roommate, you should both look at the arrangement upon which you are embarking as if it were a mine field. Take precautions so that you forge a path through the mines, eliminating the possibility of tripping off explosions.

Written Agreement

The first thing you must do is decide who is responsible for what: whose name is going on the lease and the various utility bills. Get promises all around that no one will use another's private phone line or that if everyone uses one phone, each caller will pay for his own long distance calls. Also make sure everyone understands when each roommate's share of the rent is due, and that it must be paid to the lease-holder on or before that date each month.

WRITE AN AGREEMENT COVERING

- Lease/Rent
- Utilities
- Phone—Long Distance
- Chores
    - Individual
    - Group

Also determine what actions or failures on the part of one will be just cause for the others to demand that person leave. Write out a contract outlining these agreements, make copies for everyone, and have everyone sign them, thus avoiding possible misunderstandings.

Work out a weekly schedule delegating chores such as vacuuming, dusting, floor mopping, toilet cleaning, and dish washing, so that everyone knows exactly what she or he is to do and when. Decide what sort of messes, such as scrubbing the bathtub and washing late-night snack dishes, are to be cleaned up by the individual who made them. Decide what chores can be group activities—perhaps the weekly house-cleaning. Post this weekly schedule somewhere visible, such as the refrigerator or on a tack board next to the wall phone.

Finally, work out some informal "rules of conduct." Decide how you want to handle it if any of the roommates wishes to have a late night or overnight guest of the opposite sex. If there's only one television, decide how you will determine which shows to watch. If one of you is a music major, determine what hours of the day it is convenient for the musician to practice.

VERBAL UNDERSTANDING

Guests
Overnight Guests
TV Schedule

Possible Problems

Sometimes things do get bad. My son had a roommate, an old friend from high school, when he first moved into an apartment. My son was never neat, but this other fellow was not just a slob, he was dirty. He never cleaned up after himself. He quit going to school and he quit working, too. He had all day to eat my son's personal groceries, but he never had a dime to pay his share of the bills. Things went from bad to worse when he started making lengthy, long-distance phone calls that were billed to my son and for which he never paid. He even had the nerve to invite another person into the apartment as a third roommate.

My son had to kick his (former) friend out. It wasn't easy to do, but the lease and utilities were all in my son's name. He had to use half a semester's tuition money to pay off the bills his old buddy had run up but couldn't—or wouldn't—cover. And in order to keep this fellow out, my son paid to have the locks on his apartment doors changed.

Relationships between roommates don't usually deteriorate so drastically, especially those that start out as a friendship. But if you see it coming, don't delay ending this joint tenancy quickly. If the lease or utility bills are in the names of anyone but the offending deadbeat, the other roommate is ultimately going to be responsible for them. The longer you delay, the higher the price you are going to pay.

The Problems of Food

Personal experience has led me to the conclusion that one of the biggest sources of conflict between roommates is food. When I was young and first lived in a house with roommates we tried to shop, cook, and eat communally. Every day someone was responsible for shopping and cooking for the entire household. The problem was, one person would make a tasty, ample meal of fried chicken, mashed potatoes, string beans and cherry pie, while another would open a couple of cans of stew. It wasn't fair in terms of cost or quality. Eventually we decided to shop and cook for ourselves. But far too often I would go into the refrigerator and find only the heel of my loaf of bread, or just half of my two pounds of hamburger. Much of that remaining meat would be inedible because the package had been opened and never rewrapped.

To avoid food fights, as it were, I suggest that you never "go communal." Oh, if you decide on a Saturday afternoon to go shopping together and then cook a big spaghetti dinner with salad, bread and homemade cake, that's fine. Enjoy! But let it be a spontaneous and mutually agreed upon event. Otherwise shop, cook and clean up after yourselves on an individual basis, and mark your food. Unless you have real creeps for roommates (I did), it is often unintentional that someone uses your bread or ketchup or macaroni and cheese instead of his own.

SUGGESTION FOR IDENTIFYING FOOD
Use colored-coded stickers designed to mark file folders.
Or, use white labels and initial them.

The bottom line with roommates is, you must be considerate.

- ✔ Don't spend an hour hogging the tub when you know your roommate must shower before leaving for work in twenty minutes.
- ✔ Don't leave dirty pots in the sink so that your roomie has nothing to cook in if she or he doesn't wash what you dirtied.
- ✔ Don't spend the evening making out with your current love interest on the living room floor so that your roommates are (a) unable to watch television, (b) talk on the telephone, (c) walk past to use the bathroom.
- ✔ Know when the rent and other mutual utility bills are due and give who ever is handling the bills your share of the money on time.
- ✔ Rule of thumb is, consider how you would feel if you were on the other end of whatever it is you are dishing out.

Summary

- ✔ Roommates are usually an economic choice.
- ✔ Conflict is normal. How it is handled is what's important.
- ✔ Write an agreement covering the major aspects of living together, especially the financial ones.
- ✔ Discuss other possible areas of conflict.

- ✔ Be considerate of your roommate and expect consideration in return.

Recommended Reading

Heine, Arthur J. *Surviving After High School: Overcoming Life's Hurdles*. Virginia Beach, VA: J-Mart Press, 1991.

SSS...

SAFE SEX

If you are not already sexually active, you probably will become so in the not-too-distant future. Unfortunately, these days the traditional, formerly harmless, cat-and-mouse rituals of pursuit, surrender and conquest are as dangerous as Russian Roulette. Today sex, especially (but not limited to) promiscuous sex, can result not only in unplanned pregnancies but in sickness and premature death.

No matter what your sexual orientation, sexually transmitted diseases (STDs) are rampant these days. The old standbys, syphilis and gonorrhea, are still with us, but we also have new, incurable and fatal diseases such as herpes and AIDS. Ironically, too, though very effective methods of birth control have been available for the last quarter century, the number of unwanted pregnancies and illegitimate births continues to rise, especially among teenagers.

Your parents' Free Love generation is gone; love is no longer free, and its price may be your death. Now when you "sleep" with someone, you must consider that you are "sleeping" with everyone else your partner has ever been with—a strange concept, but true. Doctors say among themselves: "AIDS will kill you, but herpes is with you for the rest of your life." The only 100% effective precautionary measure you can take to prevent disease and unwanted pregnancies is celibacy.

In lieu of celibacy, sexually active people must protect themselves and their partners. Become knowledgeable. Find out all you can about sexually transmitted diseases and how to prevent unwanted pregnancies. As far as diseases go, learn how to prevent them, what the symptoms are, what the treatment (if any) may be. Don't ask friends for the answers unless they are experts. Take the time to visit your doctor, a medical clinic or even a library to get the information you need.

In a nutshell, you should never engage in sexual intercourse without protection. This means the man must wear a condom. This is the only form of protection, other than celibacy, against STDs for both partners. If a woman is using some kind of birth control (The Pill, an intrauterine device [I.U.D.], or a diaphragm) and the man uses a condom, there will be even less chance of pregnancy. No temporary birth control method is 100% effective; using two forms of protection increases your safety.

After becoming familiar with the symptoms of sexually transmitted diseases, if you notice any of these symptoms, seek medical attention immediately. Some initial symptoms eventually pass. That doesn't mean the disease has run its course. It only means it has become dormant and will manifest itself later—possibly years later with other symptoms.

Today many of these diseases can be treated, resulting in a complete cure. Genital herpes can't be cured, but it is believed to be contagious only during flare-ups.

Be honest with your partner. If you contract herpes, don't sleep with someone without telling your potential partner. Even if you are not contagious at the time, your partner has a right to know the risks. If you are afraid of being shunned or rejected, associate intimately only with others suffering from the same malady. There are now organizations for people infected with herpes.

Know your partner well. The era of one-night stands should be over. Since doing a blood stick in a bar on a new acquaintance hasn't become standard practice, it is best for you to get know a person very well before becoming intimate. Courting and being courted isn't a bad thing. It can be sweet, romantic and wonderful. Making love with someone you know, desire and care for is far more satisfying than sex with a stranger.

Summary

Practice safe sex. It prevents both pregnancy and disease.

Recommended Reading

Woods, Samuel G. *Everything You Need to Know About STD—Sexually Transmitted Diseases.* New York: The Rosen Publishing Group, 1990.

Johnson, Earvin "Magic." *What You Can Do to Avoid Aids.* New York: Times Books, 1992.

SSS...

TTT...

TAXES

There's an old saying: "The only sure things in life are death and taxes." Hopefully, death is far in your future. But taxes are immediate. Their time is now.

Filing your federal income tax may seem like a scary thing. Lots of people draw a blank when it comes to understanding and doing their own taxes. But you most likely have a relatively simple tax situation and will be able to understand and complete your own tax returns. Later, when you are making gobs of money and your tax situation is much more complicated, you will be able to understand what your tax accountant is talking about.

This chapter will give you some of the basics. You will need to fill in the blanks by referring to the Internal Revenue Service (IRS) instruction booklet sent with your tax form, having telephone discussions with an IRS information office, and getting advice from people you trust who have been doing their own taxes for some time.

Federal Income Tax Filing Forms

The first thing you will need to know is which federal income tax form (1040EZ, 1040A, or 1040) to file. Chances are that most of you reading this book will qualify to use the 1040EZ form.

Each tax instruction booklet sent out by the IRS with federal income tax forms contains a list of who is qualified to use each of the three 1040 forms. For you, the most important (but not all) qualifications for using to use the 1040EZ are:

- ✔ You were single at the end of the taxable year
- ✔ You had no dependents
- ✔ You don't itemize deductions or claim any adjustments to income or tax credits

If it is your first time to file taxes or you have moved since the last time you filed, you will *not* receive a tax booklet in the mail. Call the IRS forms number (1-800-TAX-FORM) to have a booklet sent to you or check with your local library, bank, post office or IRS office. Do this as soon as possible because the local library, bank and post office may run out of forms. You will also need to do this if your tax situation has changed and you need a different form than the one you received in the mail.

Remember to read the tax booklet that comes with your tax form.

To Itemize or Not to Itemize

If your actual itemized deductions are greater than the standard allowable deduction, then it is probably worthwhile for you to itemize. If you determine that it is worthwhile to itemize, you will have to use form 1040 and Schedule A which is found in the same instruction booklet with the 1040 form. Each year the federal government establishes new standard deduction amounts. For example, in 1992 the standard allowable deductions were as follows:

YOUR FILING STATUS	YOUR STANDARD DEDUCTION
Single	$3,600
Unmarried Head of Household	5,250
Married Filing Jointly	6,000
Married Filing Separately	3,000

There is a very good chance that itemizing deductions will not be practical for you. For a single person, the standard deduction is $3,600. So you would need actual, allowable deductions greater than $3,600 for itemizing deductions to be of benefit to you. Unless you are buying a home and have substantial interest and property tax deductions, the standard deduction amount will be difficult to exceed. However, always consider this an option and check out whether it would be an advantage to you.

How Many Exemptions to Claim

When you first started your job, your employer should have asked you to fill out a W-4 form to indicate how many exemptions you intend to claim. The W-4 includes a worksheet to help you determine the correct number of exemptions to claim. By submitting a W-4 form, you are authorizing your employer to withhold federal (and state) income tax from your wages and submit the tax to the IRS (and state) on your behalf.

If you end up owing $500 or more in tax and the amount owed the IRS is more than 10% of the total tax you should have paid, you may owe a penalty. Obtain form 2210 to see if you owe a penalty and to figure the amount. To avoid this penalty be sure that your employer is withholding the correct amount for you by indicating the proper number of exemptions. If you are single with no dependents, you should probably claim only one exemption.

There are three conditions (on the W-4 form) which must be met to qualify for tax exempt status. Be sure that you meet all three conditions before you indicate this status.

Why would anyone claim fewer deductions than they are allowed? After all, most of us think the IRS takes too much of our earnings as it is. But some people claim fewer dependent deductions than they are entitled because it ensures them a refund. They look at it as forced savings. It's an expensive savings plan. The government takes your money all through the year and uses it without paying you interest. A far better plan is to declare only your legitimate exemptions and methodically set aside any extra cash you can spare for investing.

A Caution About 1099s/Contract Labor Status

A 1099 is the form which an employer will send to you and the IRS at the end of the year if you were simply paid an amount of money for work performed and no taxes were withheld from the amount you were paid. You may very well receive legitimate 1099s from employers. But beware.

Some employers like to classify workers as contract labor so that they will not have to pay their share of Social Security tax or make withholding tax deposits to the IRS for the employee. There are strict guidelines for classifying workers as contract labor and not many employers can justify doing it. Be sure that you are properly classified for tax purposes. The result of being paid as contract labor is that you will be responsible for paying all the tax which was not withheld throughout the year including Social Security tax which you will then have to pay at a higher self-employment rate.

If you go to work for an employer who doesn't deduct any taxes from your paycheck, inquire about it right away. Although you may report this employer to the IRS, the IRS ultimately holds you responsible for any tax liability.

Getting Ready to File Your Tax

Sometime prior to April 15th gather all your necessary tax forms and documentation. You will be responsible for the documentation whether you or a tax preparer does your tax. This may include the following:

- ✍ Your tax forms and IRS instruction booklet
- ✍ W2 and 1099 earnings statements

If you itemize:

- ✍ Medical and dental payment records
- ✍ Real estate and personal property tax receipts
- ✍ Home mortgage interest payment records
- ✍ Records of child care payments
- ✍ Charitable donation documentation

Tangible items such as clothes, appliances, and books, donated to a charitable organization may be used as a charitable deduction. Get a receipt for your donation and a value if possible. If the organization receiving the donation will not assign a value, be sure that you assign a fair market value (a realistic amount the articles could be sold for) to the donated items.

FORMS OF DOCUMENTATION

Canceled checks, check copies or check carbons

Receipts for deductible expenses, especially for those you may have put on a credit card such as medical expenses or business travel not reimbursed by your employer.

Free Tax Assistance

- ✔ IRS Tax Publications (1-800-TAX-FORM). Publication 910 Guide to Free Tax Services includes a list of all IRS tax publications.

- ✔ IRS Recorded Tele-Tax information. Simply call the appropriate number for your city or state and ask for the subject by topic number. The phone numbers and topic numbers are listed in your tax instruction booklet.
- ✔ Talk directly with an IRS representative. These numbers are also listed in your tax instruction booklet.
- ✔ Your local Society of Certified Public Accountants will usually offer free tax assistance to people whose income falls below a certain amount. Give them a call to find out if the service is offered and if you qualify. All you need is to have all the pertinent documentation available and a qualified accountant will take care of the rest.

How Long Should You Keep Your Tax Records?

Keep copies of all your tax records including forms, W2 and 1099 wage statements, receipts and canceled checks for at least three years from the date of filing your tax. The IRS may audit three years back for any reason. If the IRS suspects fraud, you may be audited going back as far as seven years. If you are self-employed or you freelance your services, it is best to keep records for the longer period because the IRS looks at the self-employed closer than a regular wage earner.

Summary

- ✔ Keep adequate records throughout the year.
- ✔ Make sure your employer deducts the right amount of tax from your wages by claiming the correct number of exemptions on your W-4.
- ✔ File your tax no later than midnight of April 15th to avoid penalties.
- ✔ Don't forget state tax if applicable.
- ✔ Take advantage of all the free tax help available.

Recommended Reading

———. *H & R Block, Inc. Tax Guide*. New York: Collier Books, annual.

———. *The Ernst & Young Tax Guide*. New York: John Wiley & Sons, Inc., annual.

UUU...

UNDER, OVER, ABOVE, AND AROUND

Refrigerators

There are some things other than people that need space. For example, a refrigerator should be placed so that there are a few inches between its backside and the wall to provide air circulation for the coils. Though people often put things on their refrigerators, using the top of a refrigerator for shelf space isn't the best idea. A refrigerator gets very warm on top because, as the inside of the unit cools, the heat it expels rises.

Ovens

A microwave oven needs space, too, particularly behind and at the sides. Be sure there is plenty of room for air circulation around it.

People sometimes like to store things in their conventional ovens. If you have a gas stove with a perpetually burning pilot light, that's not a good idea. The subtle warmth will make the frosting on your donuts run and might melt the plastic bread bag. Even if you have an electric oven, it is very easy to forget you stashed something inside it. Then, when you turn the oven on to preheat, you can have a messy, toxic disaster inside.

VCRs

Often, a VCR is stored on top of the television set to which it is connected. It's easy to put a can of soda or beer on top of the VCR when you get up to answer the phone, and sometimes you think your plants would look quite nice sitting there. Don't do it. VCRs get very warm while in use, so they are vented. If you place something atop them that is moist, damp, or filled with liquid, moisture could dribble into the vents and wreck your machine.

Video And Audio Tapes

Video and audio tapes can be ruined by excessive heat or cold. Don't leave them in your car, especially at the height of winter or summer. Even if it is comfortably warm outside, the inside of a car can be hot as a furnace if closed up and parked in the sun. Speaking of sun, don't leave your tapes near a window even inside your home. Sunlight can create intense heat in its direct path. Conversely, in the winter the coldest place in your house is near a window glass, especially at night. Beware, too, of heating vents and radiators.

Space Heaters

If you use a portable space heater, use caution. A lot of fires are caused by misused or neglected space heaters. These items require a lot of space around them on all sides. Keep them on the floor, out of the line of traffic. Make sure there is nothing nearby that could catch fire or melt down, things like newspapers, plastic laundry baskets, window curtains. Even tables and chairs should not be close, for wooden legs have been known to scorch and actually burn when furniture is left in close proximity to a space heater. Never leave a space heater unattended.

Fans

Oscillating fans should be given their own space, too, especially if there are children or small pets nearby. Curious kittens and toddlers may put their paws or fingers between the wire cage protecting the blades, and the result can be disastrous.

Computers

Computers and word processors require air space on all sides. Like VCRs, they get very warm while in use so they are vented. Drips and dribbles of water, coffee, soda—any liquid—can wreak havoc on their inner workings.

Bathtubs

Keep everything away from your bathtub except shampoo and soap and safety razors. Don't perch a radio on the tub's rim while you are bathing. Especially in small bathrooms, be careful that curling irons, hair dryers and electric shavers are not balanced on the edge of the sink. Should they fall into the tub while you are soaking, you will be fried.

Summary

- ✔ A lot of appliances require adequate air space around them. Microwave ovens, computers and refrigerators should have a couple of inches of room on all sides.
- ✔ Space heaters and fans can be dangerous. Never leave them unattended especially if there are small pets or children around. Keep space heaters away from anything that might catch fire.
- ✔ VCRs and computers are sensitive to moisture. Don't set beverage cans or plants on the top of or near them.
- ✔ Never bathe with small electric appliances plugged in anywhere near the tub.

U U U . . .

VVV...

VEHICLES, BUYING NEW OR USED AND SELLING

Great aunt Gertie died and left you a bundle. Well, at least enough for a sizable down payment on a car—a new car. You have had your eye on a sharp model ever since it came out, and now Fate has bestowed upon you the means to make it yours. Checkbook in hand, you hurry over to the nearest dealership.

If you are smart, you will take your father with you. Or someone who is a little older and has had some experience buying cars.

Buying A New Car

If you don't have a father or older, wiser friend to accompany you, the first thing you must do is rein in your enthusiasm. You don't want to go bounding into a new car showroom, grinning ear to ear and pointing, "I want that one." Let the salesperson court you, not the other way around.

SHOWROOM PRESENCE
Be cool
Be skeptical
Ask questions
Get all the facts
Test drive
Comparison shop

In Mexico and other countries, bargaining over the price of merchandise is not only allowed, it is a ritual. No vendor would expect a customer to accept his first stated price. This, however, has never been the custom in the United States, except when it comes to car buying. In this arena, you must negotiate like a seasoned horse-trader. Where do you begin?

You know exactly what you can afford, for a down payment, and as monthly installments on a loan. This is the most you can pay. Keep your financial boundaries firmly drawn. Be aware of them, but don't confide them to the salesperson.

Don't mention your trade-in vehicle until after you have a firm price without it.

Never let the salesperson rush you. Your impulse—and the salesperson knows it—will be to buy after a successful test drive. Instead do your bargaining, get a bottom line price in writing, but don't finalize the deal.

To bargain to a bottom line price, begin by obtaining a total cost including price, prep, licensing and registration. Next, factor special manufacturer and dealer incentives: rebates, first-time buyer programs or limited offer cash back refunds. Then, start eliminating options you were considering but don't really need: a compact disc player—you have plenty of tapes; air conditioning—you live in Minneapolis where it's hot just ten weeks a year. Only now, if you have a vehicle you could use as a trade-in, should you mention it. You will get something for that clunker, no matter what shape it is in. A car sold for scrap metal will still fetch at least $100, which can be deducted from the purchase price of a new car.

This business may sound fairly simple, a classic case of give-and-take. But it's not as easy as it sounds. The salesperson is going to get up, supposedly to talk to the manager to see if the figure you two are kicking around is acceptable. In truth, the salesperson will go to the restroom or grab a cup of coffee. It's part of the game. Then, the salesperson will return and you will continue bargaining. You will get squeamish thinking of parting with that down payment money and the burden of future loan payments. The salesperson will tell you that at the price offered, the dealer is going to lose money. Don't fall for that. No dealer is going to sell a car at a loss.

- ✔ When you get the price you can live with, get it in writing.
- ✔ Get other commitments in writing also.
- ✔ Draw an ink line through blank spaces in the contract.
- ✔ Don't put any money down now.
- ✔ Go home, think it over and make your final decision.

After you have made the decision to buy, you can go to your bank or your credit union to obtain a car loan or you can opt to finance through the car dealership. Neither financing method is better than the other unless one form offers a better interest rate. As soon as possible after deciding to buy, return to the dealership and the salesperson with whom you were negotiating. Now you will either order the car you want in the color of your choice and with the options you desire, or you will purchase the on-the-lot car you test drove.

Options

After writing out a check for the down payment you will be presented with a flurry of options that can still add to the purchase price of your new car—extended warranties, rust proofing, insurance. Extended warranties are costly and remain valid only if you have all maintenance and service performed at the dealership. This will keep you from going to that great, honest and reasonably priced local mechanic close to home or work. Virtually all cars are undercoated and there is no way to totally rust proof a car. Regular washings will help. By shopping around for vehicle insurance, you will surely find a better deal than that offered through a car dealer. So say no to all these sorts of options.

Financing

If you intend to finance through the dealership, you will next fill out a loan application and speak with the finance manager. Though the finance manager will automatically include term life insurance in the cost of the loan, decline it. You don't want to be paying extra each month for insurance that will pay off your car if you die. I mean really, if you are single, who cares?

In many instances where rebates are offered, an alternative is a low interest loan. The time to decide if you are better off taking the rebate or the lower interest rate is while you are working out the details of your car loan. It could go either way, so determine which course of action will cost you less in the long run and opt for it.

When you purchase a car via financing, full auto insurance for the vehicle is required. Be sure to bring proof of insurance when you go to pick up your new car. You don't want to drive uninsured for even a few minutes. Though the odds of having an accident on the way home from the dealership are small, it can happen. A man had his car totaled at an intersection near my house. He was devastated because he'd picked up his car from the showroom only that morning. Fortunately he was fully insured and he knew the vehicle would be replaced.

Buying a Used Car

Probably your great aunt Gertie didn't die and leave you a bundle. Probably if you are in the market for a new car, it is for a used car that will be new only to you. You can buy used cars primarily from three primary sources: used car dealers, new car dealers, and private owners. My advice is, stay away from the strictly used car dealers. They are, according to polls, among the least-trusted business people in America and for good reason. It isn't worth the time, effort or risk for you to search for a fair and honest used car dealer.

New Car Dealerships

You can, however, buy used cars from new car dealers. They sell trade-ins received in new car deals, and they also buy and exchange used cars at auctions. A new car dealership generally inspects the used cars it acquires and has needed repairs made. If you purchase a used car off a new car dealership's used-car lot, you can be fairly certain it will run decently. You will also be given a warranty that will protect you if it breaks down and/or requires expensive and extensive repairs within a short time after purchase. The down side of buying from a new car dealer is that even the used cars won't be too very old and therefore may be relatively costly. If you are in the market for something several years old and well under $2,000—especially if you are in the market for something very old and under $1,000—you would be better off buying from another source, a private owner.

Private Sellers

Most used cars are bought and sold through private individuals because both parties can get the best price that way. However, if you are the potential buyer of a used car, beware: Used cars are sold "as is," and you will get no written warranty. Therefore, if you find a used car you really want to buy, it may be in your best interest to have the car checked out by a competent mechanic. That service will cost you $50 or $60, but if you are advised that there are serious problems with the car, that $50 or $60 could well save you hundreds and hundreds of dollars for repairs on top of the car's purchase price.

There are things you should look for when buying a used car. Here are some:

- ✔ If the car's body has ripples, a gritty surface, or uneven paint, it may have been in a serious accident.
- ✔ While in neutral, gun the engine. Clunking or other strange noises probably mean there are bad rods or main bearings.
- ✔ Check to make sure everything works: lights (including high beams), turn signals, windshield wipers, safety belts.
- ✔ Is there too much play in the steering wheel? You shouldn't have more than a couple of inches. If the wheel is stiff, there might be front-end problems.
- ✔ Is the brake pedal stiff or does it go nearly to the floor? Spongy brakes mean bad brakes.
- ✔ While test driving a car with automatic transmission, listen to the engine. A whine denotes problems.
- ✔ Does a lot of smoke come out of the tail pipe? If so, the car is burning oil.
- ✔ Look under the car. Any damp stains on the pavement? Perhaps break fluid, antifreeze or oil is leaking.
- ✔ Check the belts and hoses for wear.
- ✔ Bounce both the front and back end of the car. If it keeps on bouncing after you stop pushing, the shock absorbers are worn.

It is doubtful that any used car you buy is going to be in perfect condition. The newer the car and the more it costs, the better its condition should be. Let's face it, you can't expect a ten-year-old car selling for $800 to be of the same quality as a two-year-old car selling for $6,000. Still, you should know what you are getting. Here are some other tips:

- ✔ Never buy a car you have only seen at night. A lot of flaws are hidden by darkness. Be sure you check it out in the daylight before you make an offer to purchase.
- ✔ An older car with low mileage is a better deal than a newer car with high mileage.
- ✔ Think twice when you are considering either an uncommon foreign car or one no longer being manufactured. Though the asking price may be a deal, will you be able to get parts and will those parts be affordable?

As an adult who should have known better, I once bought a used Audi. Money was tight, I needed another car, and the price was great. But I couldn't afford to maintain it. The red plastic gel to replace a cracked taillight cost $75; a new muffler system cost about $450—and this was nearly ten years ago. What originally seemed like a terrific deal turned out to be a money pit I couldn't afford.

OTHER PLACES TO BUY USED CARS

Car rental companies
Auctions
Local police impound sales
US. government agencies

There are other places to buy used cars. Among them are car rental companies, which sell their vehicles when they are one to two years old. You will be looking at newer, more expensive used cars here, but you will receive a very extensive warranty, not unlike those given for brand new cars. Another place is car auctions run by various government agencies. Local police departments may sell impounded vehicles and those towed but never claimed. Even the US. Government sells used cars, some of them Department of Transportation vehicles that were used for testing and have as little as a hundred miles on them.

Selling Your Car

When it comes time for you to sell your car, you have two basic options: Use it as a trade-in if you are buying another car from a dealer or sell it yourself. You will make more money if you sell it yourself.

To determine a selling price, look in your local newspaper classifieds to see how much others are asking for cars of a similar age and style. Go to the library and look up the "going" price in the National Automobile Dealers Association guide to car prices or the Kelley Blue Book. Then be honest with yourself. You know what is right or wrong with your car. Decide what you believe is a fair price, then:

- ✔ If there are minor repairs to be made, make them.
- ✔ Clean out the inside of your car and polish up the outside.
- ✔ Place an ad in the newspaper classifieds.
- ✔ Stick up "For Sale" notices at school or in grocery stores.
- ✔ Put a "For Sale" sign with your phone number on it in a back side window of the car itself.
- ✔ When prospective buyers come out to look at your car, answer any questions they have honestly.
- ✔ Be prepared to negotiate. No one expects to pay your asking price. Even if they can only "talk you down" by $25 or $50, they will expect to do that. You must expect to do that, too.
- ✔ When you make a deal and money changes hands, you will have to sign your title over to the buyer. In some states when you sell your car, you must record the odometer reading on the title. In other states you must get an odometer statement form from the DMV. In any case, the paperwork must be handed over to the buyer upon sale.

If you have a potential buyer who must obtain financing, get a non-refundable deposit of about $100 and agree, in writing, to hold the car for this buyer for a specified period. If you hold the car without a deposit and the potential buyer never returns with the funds to buy, you could be turning away buyers who indeed have the resources to pay. That would be foolish. If you hold the car and the deposit but the potential buyer doesn't return, you don't have to return the deposit, thus you are compensated for time lost and other buyers you rejected. However, should the buyer return in the agreed upon time with cash in hand, the deposit must be deducted from the purchase price.

Summary

- ✔ Take your time and visit more than one dealership.
- ✔ Refuse to be pushed into buying options you don't need.
- ✔ Negotiate a bottom line purchase price, get it in writing, and then go home to think on it.
- ✔ When you make the decision to buy, arrange financing through your bank or the dealership.
- ✔ Don't purchase extended warranties and extra rust proofing.
- ✔ Don't buy term life insurance added on to a car loan.
- ✔ When you are pretty certain you want to buy a particular used car, have a mechanic check it out first.
- ✔ When you are selling a car yourself, determine a fair price by looking at prices of similar used cars for sale in the newspaper classifieds.
- ✔ Clean your car, fix minor problems and then put an ad in the newspaper.
- ✔ Be sure you have the title and other required paperwork that must be signed and passed on to the buyer.

Recommended Reading

Sachs, Leslie R. and James S. Bennett. *Cheap Wheels: The Complete Guide to Buying, Selling and Enjoying Used Cars.* New York: Pocket Books, 1989.

WWW...

WARRANTIES

A warranty, in either total or partial fashion, guarantees a product. With a warranty the manufacturer is saying, "Our product is good and it will work satisfactorily for a reasonable period of time, provided it isn't misused." This pronouncement is backed up by the company's promise to repair or replace its product should it fail for any reason other than abuse. Warranties are available for almost every mechanical or electronic product, from automobiles to sewing machines to watches.

On expensive items such as new automobiles, the dealership keeps track of the warranty period. If the door handle of your new car falls off three months after you purchase it, you simply return to the dealership and have it replaced at no cost. As time passes, the terms of the warranty will change. In the case of cars, it will no longer be "bumper to bumper 100%," but "bumper to bumper" with a $100 deductible for every repair or some other variation. Eventually the warranty coverage will lapse altogether. When a car is seven years old, for example, despite the fact the owner has maintained the car according to manufacturer's instructions for the entire period, whatever goes wrong with it is the owner's responsibility. Still, some things like a catalytic converter may be covered for the life of the car.

On less expensive items—clocks, phones, CD players—the purchaser receives a warranty card when the appliance is bought. The warranty card must be filled out and mailed back to the manufacturer in order for the warranty to be in effect. If you don't do this, your appliance will not be covered under warranty. So if your six-month-old clock's alarm fails to go off when you set it or your telephone crackles when you place calls, you will be out of luck. Your only recourse will be to buy a replacement clock or phone.

In the excitement of getting a new stereo or television or dishwasher, it is easy either to forget or decide not to bother with completing and mailing warranty cards. Send in those cards. Then if you do have problems, you are not stuck with repairs for which you must pay out-of-pocket.

Basic manufacturers' warranties are great. Even if they don't cover total repairs after a certain period, they will still cover partial costs of repairs. The warranties don't cost you anything extra, just a few minutes of your time and a stamp, so take advantage of them.

But there are also extended warranties. These may be available from the manufacturer or the store where you made your purchase. These do cost money. I feel that in many instances they don't benefit the consumer.

DISADVANTAGES OF EXTENDED AUTO WARRANTIES

You are obliged to continue to take your vehicle to the dealership for all maintenance and repairs.

All maintenance work must be done according to a very specific schedule or the warranty is void.

Auto dealerships are usually more expensive for maintenance and repair work.

In some instances, you may not have the product a very long time. A prime example of this is car stereos, speakers and tape players. Not a single store sells car stereos without offering various extended warranties. Most people buying car stereos are buying them for older cars. Ask yourself, What are the odds I'll still own my car five years from now?

I have a son who didn't ask himself that question. He took his high school graduation money and laid out the big bucks for a great sound system—with extended warranties—and had it installed in his old beater of a car. This was in June. By January needed repairs far exceeded the total value of his car, he didn't make them and couldn't use the car. While it sat outside his apartment building waiting to be rolled down the hill to a nearby junk yard, someone broke into it and stole the stereo. So much for the value of his extended warranty.

On the other hand, some inexpensive extended warranties are worth the price. My other son received a watch for Christmas. It was far from a Rolex but not a rubber watch, either. It cost a little under $100. A one-year warranty came with the watch. When he filled out the card he decided to buy an extended five-year warranty that cost about $5. Sure enough, when the watch was a little more than a year old it stopped running. He went to the store, picked up a preaddressed "mailer," put his watch inside along with his warranty number, and dropped it into the mailbox. Within a couple of weeks it was returned, in perfect running order, and all he had to pay was postage.

Of course, he could have lost the watch long before the extended warranty had expired. Or he might have dropped it and stepped on it, causing non-covered damage because of "misuse." But considering the low cost of the extended warranty and the odds he would have the watch for several years, investing in the additional coverage seemed reasonable and proved itself worthwhile.

Summary

- ✔ Warranties are the manufacturer's product guarantees.
- ✔ Take advantage of all free warranties.
- ✔ Send in the warranty cards to the manufacturer.

✔ Don't automatically purchase extended warranties. Consider cost, what you get and what you will need to do to keep the warranty valid.

Recommended Reading

Sloane, Leonard. *Book of Personal Finance.* New York: Times Books, 1992.

XYZ...

GRAB BAG

You thought all the information I have provided thus far was a miscellaneous potpourri? Here comes the grab bag of all grab bags, a plethora of handy if slightly bizarre tidbits, not unlike those provided by Emily Post, Heloise, and *Consumer Reports*. I thought they might be useful, and as the rest of the alphabet has already been taken, here they come under XYZ:

You need to put a screw into the wall, but have no drill

Take a nail with a shaft roughly equal in diameter to the screw (slightly narrower will do, but no larger). Pound it into the wall, then remove the nail and screw your screw into the nail hole.

You have bread in a plastic bag but no twist tie

The end keeps falling open and the loaf gets hard and stale? Twist the end of the bag only once or twice. Then take the excess plastic beyond the twist and fold it back, like the petals of an opening flower. Pull the excess wrapper back over the end of the loaf. It will stay put, the twist will keep air from penetrating, and the bread will remain fresh.

Run out of glass cleaner?

A good substitute is a mixture of water and vinegar, two parts to one. If you simply spattered on the bathroom mirror and are in a hurry, sprinkle a little clean water on the mirror and then wipe clean with a dry towel.

Cooking food rare

You can eat rare beef and even some kinds of raw fish, but pork and fowl must be cooked thoroughly. If you ever prepare chicken or pork and you see that the meat is pink near the bone or find a trace of blood anywhere, pop the meat back into the oven for further cooking.

Think you ate tainted food?

If you ever fear you have eaten tainted meat or food, try to bring it up quickly. A simple method is to crack open and swallow a raw egg. Don't do this if you think you have swallowed certain poisons. Read the poisonous substance's label warnings. Some things (such as lye—"Draino") that burn flesh could cause fatal damage if you induced vomiting.

Getting wrinkles out of clothes

Do you have wrinkles in your suit and no time to take it to the cleaners to be pressed? Hang it in the bathroom while you shower. The steam will eliminate a lot, if not all, of the wrinkles.

Mortgages

If you are in the market for a condo or a house, don't opt for the old standby, a thirty-year mortgage loan. The only one that benefits from a thirty-year loan is the lender. By the time you have paid off your property, you will have repaid the purchase price three times over. Instead take a fifteen-year loan. Your installment payments will not be twice those of a thirty-year loan, only about 17% more. And in the long run, you will save yourself tens, perhaps hundreds of thousands of dollars in interest.

Getting parking tickets doesn't seem like much of a crime

Well, in the scheme of things, it's not—unless you accumulate several and don't pay them on schedule. In that case you can be arrested, jailed and prosecuted. Pay your parking tickets promptly.

Everything you put into a microwave oven comes out hard as a rock

This is far from a scientific explanation but, basically, microwave ovens work because they make the little molecules of any item zip around faster and faster, creating heat. Water molecules—moisture—are the first to get moving. When they vaporize into steam they rise and escape the food. Food without moisture is hard. The way to prevent microwaved food from getting hard is to wrap it in wax paper or special microwave paper. (Cellophane works to some degree, but if left in the oven too long it melts.) Don't overheat—especially bakery products, such as bread or pastries. A few seconds does it. The same holds true for cheese. Melting should only take a minute.

Involved in a traffic accident

If you are ever involved in a traffic accident, even a minor one, wait till the police or a sheriff arrives on the scene to write a report, particularly if the other driver is at fault. You will be in a far better position to collect for damages if she or he has been legally cited and issued a ticket.

Trust your own instincts

There is no one, from your mother to a guardian angel, who is watching your every move and will advise you if something's amiss. If you suspect the salesman is trying to pull a fast one on you, he probably is. If you are worried you are in the wrong biology class because your name is never called at roll, you probably are. If it seems there is too much or too little being withheld for taxes from your paychecks, this might well be the case. Do you have that "Uh Oh!" feeling? Pay attention to it. Be cautious or investigate or refuse to commit yourself until you get all the facts. Look out for yourself, because no one else is going to do it any longer, now that you are on your own. And if you can't trust yourself, who can you trust?

Washing tennis shoes

Cotton and rubber tennis shoes can be washed and dried in machines. Leather athletic shoes can't.

Serving alcohol at your party

If you have a party at which you serve alcohol, you are ethically and often legally responsible for your guests. You may even be held accountable if one of them, driving drunk, is involved in an accident on the way home.

Stay sober if you are hosting a party. Cut your guests off if you feel they've had too much to drink. Send inebriated guests home with designated drivers, take them home yourself, or call cabs for them. You don't want to serve prison time for being responsible (irresponsible) for a string of events that results in tragedy and subsequent legal action.

Don't stick a butter knife into the toaster

Don't stick a butter knife into a toaster slot if your bread gets stuck. At least, don't do it until you have unplugged the toaster. You could get the shock of your life.

Doing electrical work around you home

If you are doing any electrical work—trying to fix a wall lamp, or checking to see why an outlet isn't functioning—unplug the appliance or disconnect the fuse to the outlet. Otherwise, you may get the last shock of your life.

If you have to change a fuse, wear shoes with rubber soles. Don't do it barefoot or in stocking feet. And don't use pennies—use replacement fuses. Pennies may work, but they are potentially dangerous.

Living in old buildings, you may find yourself with few outlets. Don't overload outlets. Instead of sticking small, multiple outlet adapters into wall outlets, use surge protectors. (A surge protector combines an extension cord with a long box of several three-pronged receptacle electrical outlets. A flip switch automatically shuts off the power to the box if there is a potential overload.) Overloading wall sockets can precipitate house fires.

Running a fever

Should you be sick with a cold or flu, running a fever, shaking with chills, aching with sore body muscles and should you absolutely, positively have to be somewhere besides bed (like at your final exams or starring in a play), drink water—lots and lots and lots of water until you think you are going to float away.

Though copious amounts of water won't cure your ills, they will alleviate specific complaints because most of these are aggravated by dehydration. Literally swamping your body with water (not juice or soda or any liquid that must be broken down by your system, only plain water), will cause your fever to drop a couple of degrees and your aches and pains to subside enough for you to function.

When you are home with a fever, don't bundle up to sweat it out. That's a fallacy that can make you sicker. Stay as cool as you can with light covers and alcohol rubs.

Car gas tank sprung a leak?

Has the gas tank in your jalopy sprung a leak, but you have no money for welding repairs? Chew a big wad of gum and plug the leak with it. It works, and it should hold a fairly long time.

A grease fire in your kitchen

Ideally, you should have a small fire extinguisher at the ready. In lieu of that, smother the flames with salt. (I don't mean a few sprinkles from a shaker, I mean a stream poured directly from the round box.) Second choice is baking soda. Third is to drop a pan lid that can encompass the flames directly over the flames. The fire will run out of oxygen.

Bad smell in the refrigerator

Is there a bad smell in your refrigerator even though you threw out the fish you defrosted but never got around to preparing? Put an open box of baking soda at the back of a center shelf. It will absorb the bad odors. (Sprinkled in with the litter, it helps kill odors in the cat box, too.)

Coffee is tasting bitter

The coffee from your coffee maker is tasting bitter, and there's what appears to be an oil slick floating on the top of every cup of brew? Clean all removable parts of your coffee maker in soap and water; rinse well. Scrub the glass carafe with warm, soapy water, too, and rinse in clean, clear water. Then pour water into the coffee maker's reservoir, about three quarters full, as if you were going to brew a pot. But don't put ground coffee in the filter. Simply add about 1/4 cup of vinegar to the water. Run the machine through a brewing cycle, allowing the vinegar to clean out its inner workings. Dump the vinegar water from the carafe and fill the reservoir half full with clean water. Run a short brewing cycle as a rinse. Your coffee will again be restaurant quality.

House-plant care

Plants need water, sunlight and a little supplemental nourishment. If you have house plants, keep them near the windows, water them weekly, and every month or so put a squirt of liquid plant food in your watering can. If you discover any particular plant not thriving under this minimal regimen, experiment. If the leaves are turning brown at the edges, move the plant farther away from the window; perhaps it needs indirect light, even partial shade. If another plant is dry as a bone midweek, water more frequently. Conversely, if a plant's soil is very moist on watering day, skip it this time.

You may get a green thumb eventually. You may talk to or play music for your plants, give them treats like cold coffee, and/or bathe their leaves in milk. Or, you may not. In any case, remember they are living things. Remove dead leaves gently, water and feed them. If it proves too much trouble, buy plastic plants and silk flowers.

Why have a plunger?

A plunger is an inexpensive tool—a long, wooden handle capped by a rubber suction cup. It's the kind of tool you have to purchase before the need arises to use it. Buy one and keep it in your bathroom. Especially in older homes with older plumbing, toilets sometimes back up. You think routine housecleaning is bad? You have not lived until you have cleaned up after a toilet has overflowed. (They never overflow spontaneously; they only overflow immediately after being used.)

When you flush your toilet and the water in the bowl begins to spiral up toward the rim instead going down the drain, grab your plunger and stick it in the bowl. Place the rubber cup over the hole and push, release, push, release. Whatever is blocking the drain and preventing the water and waste from going down will probably be forced through by this action. The toilet will then function properly.

How to prevent moth holes in your clothes

Moths like to feast on winter woolens. Even if you have never seen a moth in your apartment, you shouldn't be surprised if, come fall, you discover a hole in the sleeve of your overcoat. Unless you live in Hawaii, where wool is never worn, or the Arctic Circle, where it's always worn, use mothballs when you pack away your winter woolens in the spring. Store them in plastic bags scattered with mothballs or with mothballs in the pockets of the garments. In the fall, air out, wash, or dry clean these wool clothes to get rid of the smell. (NOTE: Furs and leathers should never be stored in plastic. If you keep such items in your closet year-round, drape them in cloth. An old sheet will do.)

Things that wilt

Wilting cut flowers as well as limp lettuce and carrots can be perked up by soaking them, whole, in cold water.

Repairman and delivery services appointments

If you ever require the services of a repairman or are expecting a major delivery that can't be left outside your door in the hall, don't feel compelled to take off work or skip classes to wait at home the entire day. It is perfectly reasonable to set up an appointment time, or at least limit the time the repair or delivery person should arrive by specifying morning, afternoon, or before/after a given hour. Some repair shops are even willing to send out service people in the evenings or on Saturdays without charging extra. Sometimes you feel yourself at the mercy of others—especially repair people. But you shouldn't have to lose wages or put your grades in jeopardy because your stove needs fixing.

The importance of duplicate keys

Get at least one extra copy made of all your keys before you lose any of the originals. This means keys to your apartment, car, school locker, whatever. If you have only one key and you lose it, it will mean paying a locksmith to fashion an entire key from your lock. Such services can cost about $20 per hour. Getting a duplicate of a key you already have costs about 75¢.

Spilled something on your clothes while dining out or at a party?

Use club soda or seltzer to mop the spot. It help prevents permanent stains.

Licenses must be renewed—in most cases

(An exception is a marriage license.) If you are notified that the plates on your vehicle or your personal driver's license is about to expire, renew it before the expiration date. You can be fined for driving a vehicle with expired plates and arrested for driving with an expired license. If you are very late in renewing a driver's license, you may have to take the written and road tests all over again.

Keep important documents in a metal lockbox

If you lose your driver's license or social security card, it's not too difficult to replace them. But some documents are a real pain to replace, and even if you can obtain copies quickly, they are never the same as the originals: birth certificates, marriage licenses, baptismal records, for example. Keep such articles in a safe, lockable, preferably fireproof container. Also keep titles, deeds, insurance policies, passports and wills in the same box. If you do, your important papers will always be together and you will always know where to find them.

Deeds and titles are important. Don't toss them in a drawer with garbage disposal warranties and the receipts for your CD player or water skis. Titled and deeded properties can't be bought or sold without those titles and deeds. For instance, if you are buying a used car directly from the previous owner, you need the title signed over to you so that you can have the title put in your name and apply for license plates. A handwritten bill of sale isn't good enough.

Getting and keeping receipts

If you ever pay cash for anything or put cash down against a purchase, be sure to get a receipt. If you are making your purchase at a store or if you put $50 down on a snowmobile your neighbor is selling, get a handwritten receipt to prove you have paid in greenbacks and the seller already has your cash.

Registering With Selective Service

If you are a male and a U.S. citizen you must register with Selective Service on or around your eighteenth birthday. It's the law, and even though there is no draft at this time, you still must register. Should you receive a form from Selective Service mailed directly to your home, fill it out and mail it back. If you don't, go to the nearest Post Office and register. There are penalties if you fail to do so and are caught.

Registering to vote

If you are either male or female and a U.S. citizen, as of age eighteen you have the right to vote in both local and nationwide elections. In order to register to vote, contact your local city, village or town hall to find out when and where. Though in some states you can simply appear at the polling place for your district on election day, provide proof of citizenship and residency, and cast your vote immediately, in other states you may have to register in advance.

Selected for jury duty

Once you are a registered voter, you are eligible for jury duty. Should you ever be notified that you have been selected for jury duty, don't ignore the request. If you have work or school responsibilities that present a serious conflict, you can ask for and obtain a delay. But you must respond to the summons before requesting a postponement. If you ignore the summons to serve as a juror, it will put you outside the law.

Conclusion

No matter how many tips and how-to's I might gather and describe, whether fairly recent techniques developed to cope with the trappings of a highly technical world or age-old wisdom handed down from generation to generation, you are still inevitably going to run into situations you don't yet know how to handle.

When you do run up against something that puzzles you, no matter how trivial, ask someone older, wiser or a little more experienced for advice. You may feel embarrassed asking for instructions regarding what should be a common, ordinary activity, and the person you ask may at first seem a bit incredulous that you have to ask at all, but what we call common sense isn't an instinct we are born with. It's a collection of information and skills we acquire as we go through life. You have two ways of learning—through experimentation or by asking.

Asking is easier.

C.H.K.

INDEX

Helper: Bureaucracies Can't Help People, Only People Can

Sonja Jason   Publication date: Late summer 1993
194 pages* $12.95   ISBN 1-880197-09-X   softcover

Millions of people at some time have been, will be or are involved with two of societies most costly civilian bureaucracies, welfare and probation. There is no "average person" on welfare or probation because they come from every conceivable background. *Helper* is a series of vignettes about people and situations as seen through the eyes of the author who as a social worker and probation officer spent years working with people and the bureaucracies that were suppose to help them. The stories depict the wonder and diversity of human beings and the looniness of bureaucracies determined to fit people into rigid slots and deal with them accordingly. Sometimes the people are amusing, sometimes dangerous. *Helper* shows what doesn't work and what needs to change.

Dear Larissa: Sexuality Education for Girls Ages 10-17

Cynthia G. Akagi   Publication date: Late fall 1993
256 pages* $14.95   ISBN 1-880197-10-3   softcover

A book for mothers (fathers) to give to their daughters. It is a mother's letters to her daughter about growing up—body changes, menstruation, boys, dating, love and sex—with space for personal comments. Many parents and their children are not comfortable discussing sexuality issues. *Dear Larissa* helps parents and daughters build communication in a caring manner. A book to be read and referred to by girls ages 10 through 17.

The Power of Touch: A Guide to Healing Sexual Abuse Through Poetry Therapy

Shelly Marshall and Kiley Kiebert   Publication date: Late fall 1993
70 pages* $ 7.95   ISBN 1-880197-11-1   softcover

The Power of Touch is a powerful self-help workbook of poetry therapy designed for victims of childhood sexual abuse. The book is organized in two sections—prose and poetry which is read first and a workbook which follows. The workbook is in three sections corresponding to body, mind/emotions and spirit. The theme is validation: This happened to me; this is how I think and feel about it; this is how I become whole again.

* Page count not firm at this printing
Prices valid in the United States only and subject to change without notice.

These bestsellers are available in your bookstore or order by calling, toll-free, 1-800-828-0113 to use your Visa/MasterCard.

Mail orders must include *complete payment* (check or Visa/MasterCard number with expiration date) unless you are a government agency, college, library or another official public organization, in which case please include a purchase order number.

Included $2.00 for shipping & handling with each order. Colorado residents need to also include 3.8% sales tax.

To ensure your order is properly handled, include the name and quantity of each title, your complete name and shipping address and complete payment. Thank you.

Send orders to: GYLANTIC PUBLISHING CO.   (303) 797-6093
P. O. Box 2792   FAX 727-4279
Littleton, CO 80161-2792